THE
CUMBRIA WAY
AND THE
ALLERDALE
RAMBLE

First Published in 1997 by
Cicerone Press
Police Square
Milnthorpe
Cumbria LA7 7PY

ISBN 1 85284 242 3

Other books by Jim Watson from Cicerone Press:
Lakeland Villages
Lakeland Towns
Lakeland Panoramas

Cartoon collections:
On Foot and Finger
On More Feet and Fingers
The Walkers

Everything possible has been done to ensure that the information in this book is correct at the time of going to press. If you discover any changes please let the author know (c/o Cicerone Press) so future editions can be kept up to date. Many thanks.

HOW MUCH DO WE KNOW
ABOUT THIS GUIDE ?

THE
CUMBRIA WAY
AND THE
ALLERDALE RAMBLE
A WALKING GUIDE
JIM WATSON

*"One should always have a definite objective, in a walk as in life –
it is so much more satisfying to reach a target by personal effort
than to wander aimlessly. An objective is an ambition, and life
without ambition is ... well, aimless wandering."*

AW Wainwright
A Coast to Coast Walk 1973

CICERONE PRESS • MILNTHORPE • CUMBRIA

THE CUMBRIA WAY

THE ALLERDALE RAMBLE

Key to symbols on route maps

– – ➔ – –	Main route	– – ┤KG– –	Kissing gate
═══════	Road	– – ┤GS– –	Gap stile
– – ➔ – –	Path	– – ┤S– –	Stile
++++++++++	Railway	Bridge symbol	Bridge
ТТТТТТТТ	Fence or hedge	FB	Footbridge
∞∞∞∞∞∞	Wall	♧ ♧ ♧	Wood
▬ ▬▬▪	Buildings	⑤	Mileage
– – ┤G– –	Gate	☎	Telephone

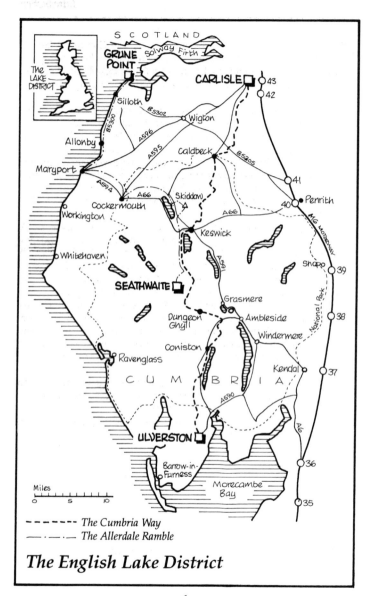

------ *The Cumbria Way*

—·—·— *The Allerdale Ramble*

The English Lake District

Compared to some long distance walks, The Cumbria Way (75 miles) and The Allerdale Ramble (50 miles) are hardly 'long' at all. But never mind the length, savour the quality. Packed into those relatively short distances is an extraordinary variety of scenery and terrain.

Most of the walking is easy, using well-established routes along the valley bottoms. If you're reasonably fit you should comfortably complete one of the walks during a week's holiday. And still have time for a day out to climb a mountain or explore a lakeland town too.

Each route can be split up into short walks to be enjoyed at different times, but by far the best way is to tackle them as a continuous day after day series of delights. That way the body and mind become more attuned to the sights and sounds of the countryside and you will feel all the better for it.

Overnight accommodation is plentiful throughout Cumbria. B&Bs are excellent value for money and welcome wet and hungry walkers. One of their breakfasts will set you up for most of the day. Central Lakeland has a good selection of camp sites and youth hostels but they are a bit thin on the ground elsewhere. Always decide where you are going to sleep before you set out and if possible book your place.

So, what about the weather? Lake District weather is notoriously unpredictable but not as bad as it's often made out. May and June are usually good walking months. September and October are not bad, especially with the spectacular autumn colours, but the days are shorter then. The wettest months according to statistics are November, December and January.

Cumbrian folklore says, 'If you can't see the fells, it's raining. If you can see the fells, it'll rain later.' Expect poor weather and prepare for terrible weather. Then you'll rarely be disappointed.

For what it's worth, I walked both routes in early June of different years and never felt a drop of rain. I hope you are as lucky.

Jim Watson

Jim Watson
Rugby, 1997

Both routes can be walked using just this guide, but for additional information and your (and the author's) peace of mind it is advisable to carry the relevant Ordnance Survey maps.

If this is your first long distance walk

1. Get fit. Walk. Start gently, building to a regular 30 minutes a day with a two to three hour walk at the weekends until you feel confident that you can walk for five or six hours at a stretch carrying a fully laden rucksack. Check with your doctor if in doubt about your fitness.

2. Cut down on sugar, fat and alcohol if you are overweight.

3. Look after your feet! Visit a chiropodist if necessary. Buy socks designed for walking. Woollen 'Loop knit' are good. Decide whether you're going to wear one pair or two pairs on the big walk. Take plenty of changes.

4. Wear in new boots. They should be lightweight and waterproof.

5. Test run your waterproofs, including trousers.

6. Plan your clothing. Remember you will have to carry all of it. Don't wear jeans. Loose fitting natural fibres are the most comfortable.

Take a hat. Especially if you're a bit thin on top!

7. Book ahead for overnight stops.

8. Be clear about the route. Read the guide and be sure you can follow all your maps.

9. Make a list of the essentials you're taking and practise packing them into the rucksack you'll be carrying. Do at least one training walk with the rucksack fully loaded. A bin liner will help to keep the contents dry in wet weather. Take a spare in case of rips.

10. Make up a simple first aid kit and learn how to use it.

11. If you are walking alone give someone a copy of your route plan for each day and your estimated time of arrival. Check in as soon as you reach your destination.

NB. You can spend a fortune buying walking kit. Consider hiring boots, waterproofs and haversack from your local outdoor shop. The quality is usually very high and the cost remarkably reasonable.

What to take

Apart from the usual day to day clothes and personal hygiene items you should include:

- Trainers and ordinary socks to change into at the end of the day.
- Maps and guides.
- Waterproofs.
- Warm midlayers. Sweaters, fleeces.
- Sunhat and sunblock in summer.
- Gloves and a woollen hat in winter.
- Basic first aid kit.
- Money. Keep it on you, not in the depths of your rucksack.
- Drinking bottle.
- Emergency rations. Chocolate is good.
- Toilet roll. (Just in case!)
- Safety pins.
- Spare bootlaces.
- Camera with lots of film.
- Whistle.
- Watch.
- List of useful phone numbers.
- Optional extras – binoculars, notebook and pen, walking stick, mobile phone (must you?).

Dogs on walks

Points for:
1. They are wonderful companions.
2. They may protect you in the highly unlikely event of you being attacked.

Points against:
1. There are few places on the Cumbria Way or Allerdale Ramble where you can allow a dog, however well trained, to run free.
2. An excitable dog will upset sheep. At lambing time they may abort their lambs.
3. The law empowers farmers to shoot dogs who worry sheep.
4. Cows are inquisitive creatures and will often follow you across a field. Ignore them and you'll come to no harm. If you have a dog with you, however, it may bark at the cows and trigger off a dangerous stampede.
5. Cows with calves are particularly hazardous. They will attack a dog, even a dog on a lead, if they think it threatens their calf.
6. The feet of dogs usually exercised in town parks may be too soft to cope with the very rough and stony terrain on parts of the routes.
7. You will have to carry dog food in your rucksack.
8. Few B&Bs accept dogs.

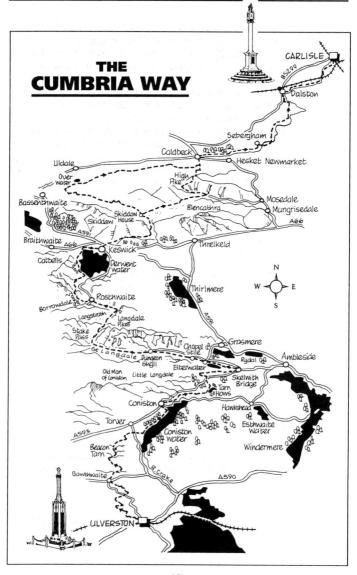

THE
CUMBRIA WAY

The 75 miles-long Cumbria Way runs northwards from Ulverston, on the shores of Morecambe Bay, to Carlisle, close to the Scottish border. It splits neatly into five sections of about 15 miles each, with overnight stops at Coniston, Dungeon Ghyll, Keswick and Caldbeck.

Overall, the route is remarkably well-balanced. Gentle farmland at both ends, a dramatic middle section amongst the high crags, and two generous chunks of classic Lakeland either side of that.

Local groups of the Rambler's Association established the Cumbria Way during the 1970s. While keeping most of the route to the valley bottoms, they also cleverly included most of the best bits of the Lake District. And in a remarkable mix of contrasts – the rolling Blawith Fells, blissful Coniston Water, pretty Tarn Hows, rugged Langdale Pikes, barren Langstrath, lush Borrowdale, regal Derwentwater, and lonely Back o' Skiddaw. The views are universally sensational.

It's easy walking most of the way, but there are three steady climbs, Stake Pass, Latrigg and High Pike, to make you feel as though you've earned all that pleasure.

Don't underestimate the Cumbria Way. To walk it is a considerable achievement. If you only ever complete one long distance walk, let it be the Cumbria Way. The satisfaction and the memories could last you your lifetime.

Maps required:
OS Landranger 1:50 000
Sheet 85 – Carlisle and the Solway Firth.
Sheet 90 – Penrith, Keswick and Ambleside.
Sheet 96 – Barrow-in-Furness and South Lakeland.
These cover all the route.
English Lakes 1:25 000 Outdoor Leisure – South West, South East, and North West sheets. These only cover the National Park area but in greater detail.

Like a definite start and end to a long distance walk? Use the war memorial at Ulverston and the market cross at Carlisle as markers.

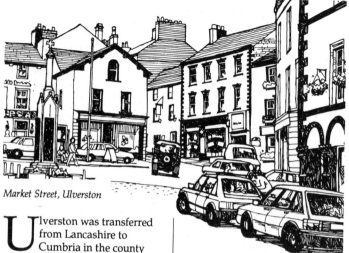

Market Street, Ulverston

Ulverston was transferred from Lancashire to Cumbria in the county reorganisation of 1974 and still retains the easy-going character of a northern market town.

Edward the First granted Ulverston a market charter in 1280. Stalls now line the cobbled streets on Saturdays. The shops are generally small and friendly family businesses. There was quite a stir recently when a modern supermarket was built in the central car park.

Ulverston expanded with the Furness Abbey iron industry, growing to a boom town with a population of over 5000 by 1840.

In 1795, John Rennie dug a mile-long canal to link the town with the sea, but after the railway arrived in 1846, sea transport became less important and trade gradually shifted to Barrow.

The industrial legacy still hangs on with Hartley's Brewery, the Cumbria Crystal glass works, a large Glaxo plant and a number of small light engineering factories, but the general impression is that the town is now content to just chug along and mop up the overflow of tourism from the Lake District.

Ulverston is notable for people who leave and become well known. Stan Laurel, who with Oliver Hardy became one of the most successful double acts in the history of show business, was born at 3 Argyle Street in 1890.

The town has a Laurel and Hardy Museum, one man's shrine to the comedy duo, set up and run by Son of the Desert, Ollie look-alike and 1974 Mayor of Ulverston, Bill Cubin. The world's

largest collection of L&H memorabilia is on display and all but two of the 105 films the pair made are continuously shown. The museum drew 15,000 visitors in 1993. Don't miss it!

Sir John Barry was born in Ulverston in 1764. He became a writer, traveller, Arctic explorer and for forty years, secretary of the admiralty. His monument, a 90ft high replica of the Eddystone lighthouse, stands on Hoad Hill overlooking the town.

Ulverston-born Lord Birkett led a famous victory in 1962 to prevent Manchester Corporation 'taking over' Ullswater and building a weir at Pooley Bridge to raise the level of the lake.

There's also little-known Maude Green. She, like Stan Laurel, left Ulverston for America. She had a son there. He grew up to become Bill Haley, the famous father of Rock 'n' Roll.

A king of comedy, a top man at the Admiralty, a saviour of the Lake District landscape and the grandmother of Rock 'n' Roll. All from Ulverston. Not bad for a town sometimes described as 'nondescript'.

Now it's time for us to leave....

WHAT TO SEE

Laurel and Hardy Museum Upper Brook Street. Tel: (01229) 582292 Open: All year, daily from 10.00.
Cumbria Crystal Lightburn Road. Tel: (01229) 584400 Glass factory and shop.
Renaissance Theatre Trust Fountain Street. Tel: (01229) 582299 Arts centre with a small coffee shop and a very good cafe.
Roxy Cinema Brogden Street. Tel: (01229) 582340
Barrow Monument Walk up Hoad Hill. Follow Hart Street into Hoad Lane and follow the path up the hill. Great all-round views.

GETTING THERE

Rail – Good service from Lancaster. Lancaster station enquiries tel: (01524) 32333
Bus – Sparse service from Ambleside via Hawkshead and Newby Bridge. Enquiries tel: (01946) 63222
Road – **A560** from **M6** Junc 36. **A6** & **A560** from Kendal. **A5084** & **A590** from Coniston.

WHERE TO EAT

Peppermill, Market Street. Tel: (01229) 587564 Good food. Reasonable prices.

The Bay Horse, Canal Foot. Tel: (01229) 53972 Gourmet. Bar meals. Fabulous views.

TOURIST INFORMATION

Coronation Hall, County Square. Tel: (01229) 587120

WHERE TO STAY

Athersmith House, 2 Casson Gdns, Ulverston. Tel: (01229) 587686

Church Walk House, Church Walk, Ulverston. Tel: (01229) 582211

Dyker Bank, 2 Springfield Road, Ulverston. Tel: (01229) 582423

The Hollies, Ford Park Crescent, Ulverston. Tel: (01229) 584458

Lonsdale House, 11 Daltongate, Ulverston. Tel: (01229) 582598

Rock House, 1 Alexandra Road, Ulverston. Tel: (01229) 586879

Sefton House Hotel, Queen Street, Ulverston. Tel: (01229) 582190

Trinity House Hotel, Princes Street, Ulverston. Tel: (01229) 587639

Virginia House Hotel, Queen Street, Ulverston. Tel: (01229) 584844

Note - This is not a recommended list. Always phone ahead with your own requirements.

CAMP SITE

Bardsea Leisure, Priory Road, Ulverston. Tel: (01229) 584712

YOUTH HOSTEL

Redhills Road, Arnside. Tel: (01524) 761781 Stay overnight and travel the 11 miles to Ulverston by train.

REFRESHMENTS

Coniston Hall: Camp site shop.
N.B. There are **no** shops or pubs between Ulverston and Coniston, and few becks for filling water bottles. **Stock up with food and drink before you leave Ulverston.**

BAD WEATHER GET-OUTS

Gawthwaite to Ulverston road.
A5092 road at Gawthwaite.
A5084 Lowick to Torver road.
Negligible bus services but you could thumb a lift in emergency.

WHAT IS IT LIKE?

A gentle start to loosen up the legs. Across farmland for the first seven miles, then a more rugged climb to the Blawith Fells and Beacon Tarn. Descent needs care in mist. The final climactic three miles are along Coniston lakeshore. Waymarking is generally poor, though there's little chance of becoming seriously lost.

BEST BIT

Torver Tarn to Coniston.

1 Ulverston to Coniston
16 miles

MAP

OS Landranger 1:50 000.
Sheet 96: Barrow-in-Furness & South Lakeland.

The start

The walk begins in the western corner of Ulverston's central car park, The Gill. A sign says 'Gillbanks. Start of Cumbria Way'.

Walk up the path for about 450 yards, then cross a stone footbridge over the beck on your left to climb out of the gill along a walled lane. At the end, turn right along an open field track marked 'Old Hall Farm'.

Through the farmyard, but just before the beck, turn left through a gap in the bridge wall. After a few strides, climb a stile over the wall on your left into the field behind the farmhouse.

Head up the hill, along the edge of the wood to the beck behind Bortree Stile. Go upstream to about 75 yards above the house, then cross the beck to a gap stile into a flat field.

The extensive view back across Ulverston and Morecambe Bay includes the Bowland Fells, the Three Peaks area of Yorkshire and the twin block towers of Heysham nuclear power station.

Continue climbing between two rocky knolls and cross two fields to the road at High Lath farm. Turn right and go down the road to Windy Ash. Here a sharp turn left along a grassy garth brings you to a huddle of farm buildings at Newbiggin. Keep on the farm road until it swings right. You should return to the fields through a gate straight ahead.

In the third field, veer left away from the wall and go through an iron gate where a wall and a hedge meet.

Keep topside of Stony Crag and cross the farm lane into the field behind the house. Follow the wall on your right to a wooden

Ulverston from above Bortree Stile

gate, prominently marked 'path', into the lower field. Turn left immediately and follow the edge of the field to Hollowmire. The route through the farmyard is clearly signed.

Keep on the farm lane. At the junction, turn left along the minor road. Where the road swings left, go through a kissing gate on your right and cross the meadows to St John's church.

Turn right along the road past the church. Coniston Old Man now dominates the northern sky. On clear days the Scafells can be seen away in the distance to the left of Dow Crag.

At the tee junction, turn left for a short distance along the Gawthwaite to Ulverston road, then turn right down a minor road to Broughton Beck. The peaceful hamlet has no shop or pub to tempt the weary walker.

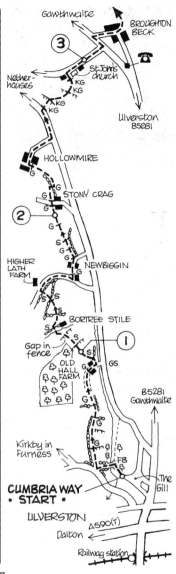

Broughton Beck

Go down the lane out of Broughton Beck and cross over a bridge. At the beck with a signpost on the other side, turn left into a field. Keep between the walls, then climb a stone step stile in the wall on your right into the next field.

Veer left to the centre of the field, cross the beck and turn upstream to a series of stiles. They lead to an unfenced road curling round a hill to Knapperthaw.

At a 'Y' junction of minor roads just beyond the farm, turn up the road on your left for a few yards, then turn right through a gate in a stone wall onto the long lane to Keldray.

Go through the metal gate and follow the footpath arrows to two stiles on your left. After climbing them, turn right to follow the wall behind the farmhouse into a steep field.

Knapperthaw

Cross the slope to a gap stile in the wall near an electricity pole. In the next field, keep left against another wall, then climb a rough lane to the hamlet of Gawthwaite.

Cross the road and swing right between the houses. Bear left at a 'Y' junction onto a hard surfaced lane between wire fences. At a right turn to High Stennerley a splendid view of the route ahead appears, undulating past Kiln Bank and Cockenskell farms to the distant Blawith Fells.

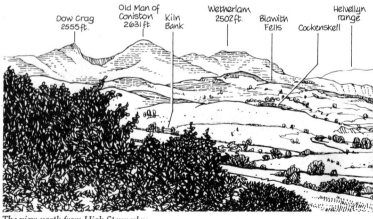

The view north from High Stennerley

Keep on the lane around High Stennerley house to the junction with a narrow walled road at the bottom. Turn right along it for about 25 yards, then go left through a gate onto rocky ground where the path is unclear.

Follow the skimpy hedge and pass through a gateway into a sloping field. Turn right down the field, go over a stile in the bottom corner and turn left up the road on the other side.

If you have difficulty finding the route here, return to the walled junction, walk down the road past Kendall Ground farm, then turn left at the first junction.

The road climbs through woodland to an open position, where the road bends right. Here, the Way goes left, climbing appropriately-named Long Lane to Kiln Bank, a lonely farmhouse with a fabulous view south.

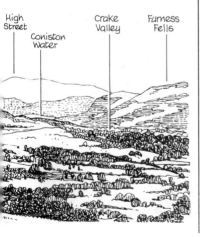

Tottlebank

Go past the farm buildings and turn right up a clearly-marked enclosed pathway beside a barn to a track going left across the low fellside. When the track divides, keep to the higher route across open country. This joins a narrow unfenced road up to Tottlebank.

About thirty yards before the farmhouse, a Cumbria Way sign indicates a green track climbing up through the bracken on your right. Bear right around the hill as you climb, then head down towards Cockenskell, the only building in sight.

Keep left of the house and go down a grassy lane enclosed by a broken-down wall to a beck. Cross by the footbridge and climb straight up the rough fellside. The path levels out for a short stretch before arriving at Beacon Tarn.

This is a good place to stop, open the sandwiches, listen to the curlews, and admire the splendid view of the Coniston fells.

The official route continues along the west side of Beacon Tarn, but it can be wet and boggy. The east side is dryer and more interesting too, picking your way between the outcrops of rock.

The surprisingly steep descent from Beacon Tarn twists down to Stable Harvey Moss, a boggy, moorland area with few clear tracks. Keep to its southern side before cutting across to join an unfenced road at a hairpin bend.

Climb for about 125 yards, then take a bridleway going off left towards a line of electricity poles. Cross the beck on your left when

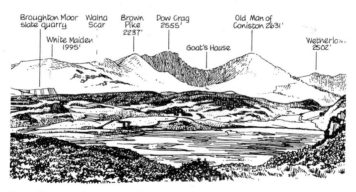

Beacon Tarn

Cockenskell

you come to it for a look at Torver Tarn, hidden in a basin of hills.

Return to the path and follow the tumbling beck down the gill to the A5084 Torver to Blawith road.

Torver, one mile left along the road, has a telephone box, an inn and accommodation, but in good weather the climax of the day's walk along the Coniston shoreline is much too good to miss.

Torver Tarn

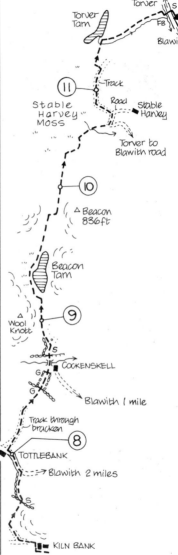

The lakeside path

Cross the road and follow the sign 'Coniston via lakeshore' onto a track which descends gently to three miles of sheer delight. The route is obvious, so you can give your full attention to the high quality surroundings.

Brantwood, the home of John Ruskin, the 18th century reformer, artist and critic, from 1872 until his death in 1900, stands across the lake, starkly white against the dark background of Grizedale Forest. Ruskin bought Brantwood without seeing the house, saying any place opposite the Coniston fells must be beautiful. Alas, the house was a ruin, but over the years Ruskin turned it into a flamboyant country mansion, now open to the public as a memorial to a remarkable man.

The Way also passes the restored, 15th century, cruck-framed Coniston Hall. Its four enormous chimneys are a landmark for miles around.

'Gondola'

You may be lucky enough to see 'Gondola' steaming across the lake. Built in 1856, she worked on Coniston until 1919.

In 1966, an admirer rescued her from the scrap heap and began a dedicated restoration. Later, a National Trust appeal raised £250,000 for a complete refit. The elegant steamboat re-entered public service in 1980.

Approaching the village from Coniston Hall

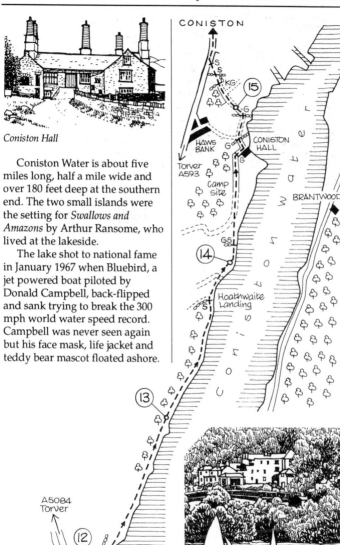

Coniston Hall

Coniston Water is about five miles long, half a mile wide and over 180 feet deep at the southern end. The two small islands were the setting for *Swallows and Amazons* by Arthur Ransome, who lived at the lakeside.

The lake shot to national fame in January 1967 when Bluebird, a jet powered boat piloted by Donald Campbell, back-flipped and sank trying to break the 300 mph world water speed record. Campbell was never seen again but his face mask, life jacket and teddy bear mascot floated ashore.

CONISTON

CONISTON HALL

HAWS BANK

Torver A593

Camp site

BRANTWOOD

Hoathwaite Landing

A5084 Torver

SUNNYBANK

Brantwood

WALK RECORD

Section 1 - Ulverston to Coniston - 16 miles

Date walked
24/2/03

Departure time from Ulverston	Arrival time at Coniston
11 40	17.30

Weather conditions
FINE WARM DAY

Notes
TRAIN 1½ HRS LATE HENCE
LATE START.
STAYED @ YEWDALE
HOTEL.

I FEEL LIKE THE OLD MAN OF CONISTON. TODAY

The Black Bull and Yew Pike

The grey slate village of Coniston can be a bit of a disappointment, but its setting, between the lake and Coniston Old Man, makes up for everything. This is a village for outdoor people, and is best seen in sunshine.

Shops are the butcher, baker, grocer type, sprinkled amongst a motley gaggle of gift shops and cafes. Now established on the Lakeland coach tour circuit, Coniston village developed with the local mining industry.

The Normans were first to mine Coniston copper. Peak output was achieved about 1860, when more than 500 men were employed. The lake was a busy waterway for 80 years, carrying iron ore to be smelted in lakeside bloomeries. Coppice plantations along the shore provided fuel. The lake became so polluted with industrial waste the fish came close to extermination.

Slate quarries were opened on the Old Man and at Tilberthwaite, attracting more workers to the village. Some came from the Mines Royal in Borrowdale. A branch line to Foxfield linked the mines to the main coastal railway in 1859.

Crown Hotel

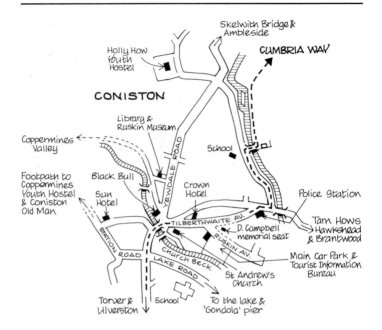

But the good times didn't last. Mining companies, who had hoped to find gold and silver as well as copper, pulled out and a steady decline set in. By 1890, mining had virtually disappeared.

The area round Church Beck above the village was intensively mined for over 300 years and is still called Coppermines Valley. One of the old mine buildings is now used as Coppermines youth hostel.

Tourists shunned the railway and the lines were torn up in 1957. The station used to be up the hill past the Sun Hotel.

Coniston's most famous resident was John Ruskin, the Victorian polymath, who lived at Brantwood from 1872 until his death in 1900. He spent most of his latter years in a wheelchair in the turret on the south-west corner of the house, gazing across the lake to the Coniston fells, the view which persuaded him to buy Brantwood in the first place.

Coniston Old Hall is the village's oldest building, built around 1250 by the area's biggest landowners, the Flemings. The National Trust bought the Old Hall in 1972 and turned the extensive lakeside grounds into a splendid camp site.

St Andrew's Church stands on a site going back to 1586. The present building, shrouded in huge conifers, was built in 1819. John Ruskin was buried here at his own request in preference to Westminster Abbey. A florid Anglo-Saxon cross carved from local Tilberthwaite slate marks his grave.

Arthur Ransome lived at the southern end of the lake and the area features prominently in his novels, most famously in *Swallows and Amazons*, which was also filmed on Coniston Water.

A green slate seat on the village green opposite the car park and information centre commemorates Donald Campbell. During his water speed record attempts on the lake, Campbell stayed at the Sun Hotel.

Turner, Wordsworth, De Quincey and numerous other arty

Yewdale Road

types preferred to stay at the Black Bull, the seventeenth century coaching inn overlooked by Yew Crag at the village centre.

Coniston attracts all kinds of visitors, but the oddest were possibly aboard a flying saucer that two local boys photographed near the village in 1954.

Tilberthwaite Avenue

WHAT TO SEE

Brantwood Eastern lakeside, 2 miles from village. Tel: (015394) 41396
Open: Mar-Nov, daily 11.00-5.30.
Ruskin Museum The Institute, Yewdale Road, Coniston.
Tel: (015394) 41541
Ruskin memorabilia. Good collection of minerals. Photographs of Donald Campbell and Bluebird.
Open: Mar-Oct, daily 11.00-5.00.
Lake trip on *Gondola* Sails Apr-Nov, daily from Coniston pier, but not in bad weather. Stops at Brantwood.
Sailing check – Tel: (015394) 41288
Evening stroll up Station Road for great fell and lake views.

GETTING THERE

Bus – Hourly service 505 & 506 from Ambleside.
Meagre service from Ulverston.
Enquiries tel: (01946) 63222
Road – A593 from Ambleside.
A590 & **A5084** from Ulverston.

WHERE TO EAT

Brantwood Brasserie.
Tel: (015394) 41396
Teas and lunches in delightful style.

Blue Bird Cafe, Coniston Boating Centre, Lake Road.
Tel: (015394) 41649

Pub grub at Black Bull, Crown Hotel and Sun Hotel. Variety of cafes.

TOURIST INFORMATION

Main Car Park, Ruskin Avenue.
Tel: (015394) 41533

WHERE TO STAY

Black Bull Inn, Yewdale Road, Coniston. Tel: (015394) 41335/41668

Crown Hotel, Tilberthwaite Road, Coniston. Tel: (015394) 41243

Sun Hotel, Station Road, Coniston. Tel: (015394) 41248

Beech Tree (veg.), Yewdale Road, Coniston. Tel: (015394) 41717

Goldberry, 3 Collingwood Close, Coniston. Tel: (015394) 41628

Hillgarth, Station Road, Coniston. Tel: (015394) 41632/41161

Lakeland House, Tilberthwaite Av., Coniston. Tel: (015394) 41303

Oaklands, Yewdale Road, Coniston. Tel: (015394) 41245

Orchard Cottage, Yewdale Road, Coniston. Tel: (015394) 41373

Note - This is not a recommended list. Always phone ahead with your own requirements.

CAMP SITE

Coniston Hall.
Tel: (015394) 41223

YOUTH HOSTELS

Holly How, Coniston.
Tel: (015394) 41323

Coppermines, Coniston.
Tel: (015394) 41261

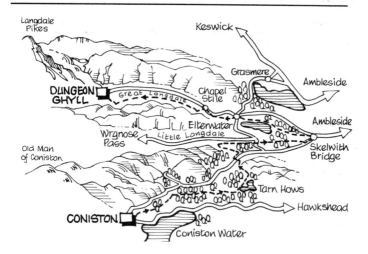

2 Coniston to Dungeon Ghyll
13 miles

MAPS

English Lakes 1:25 000. South West and South East sheets.
Or OS Landranger 1:50 000. Sheets 96 and 90.

REFRESHMENTS

Skelwith Bridge: Tea gardens.
Elterwater: Britannia Inn. Village shop.
Chapel Stile: Wainwrights Inn. Village store.

BEST BIT

Brilliant all the way!

BAD WEATHER GET-OUTS

Coniston to Skelwith Bridge: Bus service on Coniston to Ambleside road never far away.
Skelwith Bridge to Dungeon Ghyll: Road to Ambleside always close, but you may have to wait a while for a bus.

WHAT IS IT LIKE?

Begins with a steady climb out of Coniston through patches of woodland to THE popular beauty spot, Tarn Hows. Then gentle descent across mouth of Little Langdale to Skelwith Bridge. The final stretch up Great Langdale to Dungeon Ghyll is low-level Lakeland walking at its glorious best. Good pub stop at Elterwater. Plenty of variety. Great views. No hard climbs or descents. Waymarking is patchy.

Leave Coniston by crossing the stone footbridge over Yewdale Beck opposite the school. Follow the beckside path up the fields past the village football field to a wood. Half way up the hill, at a ruined byre with an ornate castle-like front, there's an excellent final view back across Coniston.

Keep on the path through a short section of wood and cross a stile into an open field beyond. Keep walking downhill to the end of the wood on your right. Cross an unfenced track and bear left through a gate in a wire fence.

Head for a ruined cottage on the other side of the field, where a stile leads to a rough lane. Turn left down the lane towards Low Yewdale farm. Just before a stone bridge, climb a stile in the wall on your right and walk along the riverbank to another stile into Tarn Hows Wood.

The path divides at the gates of a fenced enclosure in a clearing. Take the path going left. Keep climbing on a well-defined path through the wood, crossing two stiles and a wooden bridge to Tarn Hows Cottage. Just before the gate into the cottage yard, look left over the wall for a great view of Yewdale and High Yewdale farm, another calendar star, noted for its spinning gallery.

Go through the gate out of Tarn Hows Cottage yard. Keep on the lane around the top of the wood to another gate which opens onto the steeply winding road to Tarn Hows.

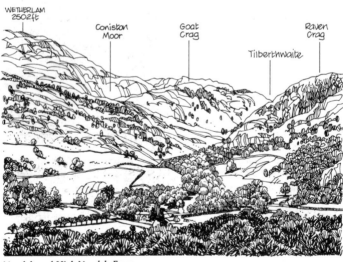

Yewdale and High Yewdale Farm

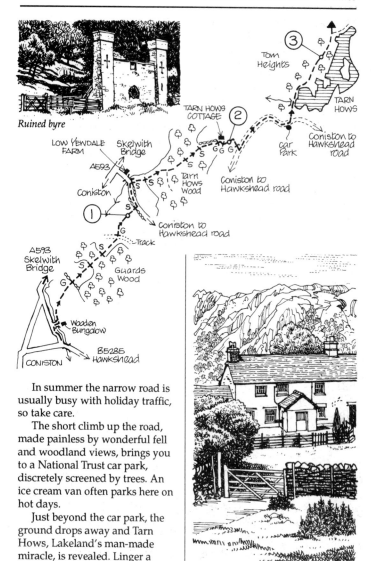

Ruined byre

In summer the narrow road is usually busy with holiday traffic, so take care.

The short climb up the road, made painless by wonderful fell and woodland views, brings you to a National Trust car park, discretely screened by trees. An ice cream van often parks here on hot days.

Just beyond the car park, the ground drops away and Tarn Hows, Lakeland's man-made miracle, is revealed. Linger a while and rejoice.

Tarn Hows Cottage

– 31 –

Tarn Hows is not your usual Lakeland tarn. This one has two car parks, public toilets and over a million visitors a year.

It was created around 1914, from a number of small pools and some marshy ground, as a landscape garden, by the Marshall family of Monk Coniston Hall. They built a dam, flooding the shallow valley to power a sawmill. Pines, larches, oaks and spruces were planted, and a circular shoreline path was made.

In 1929, the 4000 acre Monk Coniston Estate, which included Tarn Hows and much of the land today's walk crosses, was put up for sale. To prevent the estate being broken up it was bought by Beatrix Potter and sold on intact to the National Trust. The Trust still wages a constant war against erosion, planting ever more trees, building fences, footbridges and paths, and generally making Tarn Hows even more artificial.

The broad skyline of fells, however, remains just as nature intended. From here Wetherlam looks like a giant and the Helvellyn and Fairfield ranges dominate the north. But all eyes are drawn to the unmistakable profiles of the Langdale Pikes. For walkers on the Cumbria Way this is the first sighting of the Pikes. Today's stage ends at the foot of the Pikes at Dungeon Ghyll.

Though hugely popular with visitors, Tarn Hows is still thought of as a vulgar intrusion by the local literati. Writer and climber, Alan Hankinson, dismisses it as, 'the most popular parking place in Lakeland'. Norman Nicholson, Lakeland's greatest poet since Wordsworth, likened Tarn Hows to a wide screen setting for *Rose Marie*. Photographer, Cressida Pemberton-Pigott dislikes it because it reminds her of Surrey!

The view looking north across Tarn Hows

But despite the detractors, the over-planting of trees and shrubs not normally found in the Lake District, the picnickers, the radios, the swimmers, the teenage footballers and the dogs, Tarn Hows on a crisp, bright morning is a scene of rare and unforgettable beauty.

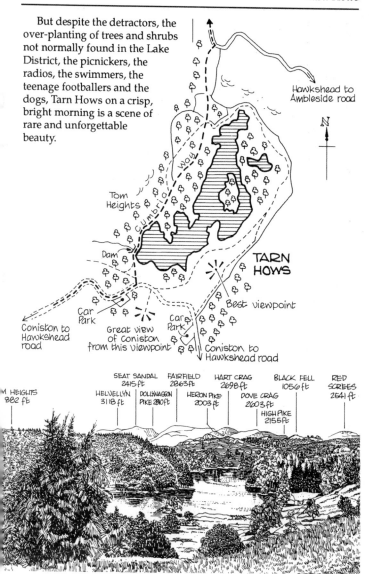

Hawkshead to Ambleside road

N

Tom Heights

Cumbria Way

Dam

TARN HOWS

Best viewpoint

Car Park

Coniston to Hawkshead road

Great view of Coniston from this viewpoint

Car Park

Coniston to Hawkshead road

M HEIGHTS 882 ft

SEAT SANDAL 2415 ft

HELVELLYN 3118 ft

FAIRFIELD 2863 ft

DOLLYWAGGON PIKE 2810 ft

HART CRAG 2698 ft

HERON PIKE 2003 ft

DOVE CRAG 2603 ft

HIGH PIKE 2155 ft

BLACK FELL 1056 ft

RED SCREES 2541 ft

The junction with the main road

Continue along the track on the west side of the tarn. Cross the dam and go through the wood to a clearing. Here, swing left down a grassy footpath to a stile onto a rough and undulating lane. Turn left up the lane. There's a great view of Windermere, framed by steep, bracken-clad hills, over the broken-down wall on your left. You are now well into real Lakeland country.

Across the main Skelwith Bridge to Coniston road, look for the footpath sign indicating a path along the field parallel to the road. Further on, return to the road for a short distance, then turn left down a narrow road signposted 'High Park'. Bear right at the fork.

High Park is a traditional 'Longhouse' farmstead, wonderfully set at the entrance to Little Langdale. Go through a gate at the right hand end of the farm yard and follow a wire fence into the wood. The 'official' Cumbria Way goes straight on, but if you want to see Colwith Force take the path going left to the river. I'd go left every time.

The two paths rejoin in a clearing overlooking a road. Cross the road and go over a stile into a field. Follow the river bank to a steep path up a wooded bank. At the top, join a track for a mile of easy walking between farms with superb views of Little Langdale on your left.

When you come into sight of the main road again on your right, leave the track and follow a path into the wood ahead. This returns you to the road near Skelwith Bridge.

Go left along the road and cross the stone bridge into the small village. Turn left straight away and walk through the stone mason's yard onto a wooded path along the river bank. Pause at Skelwith Force for photos, then

High Park Farm

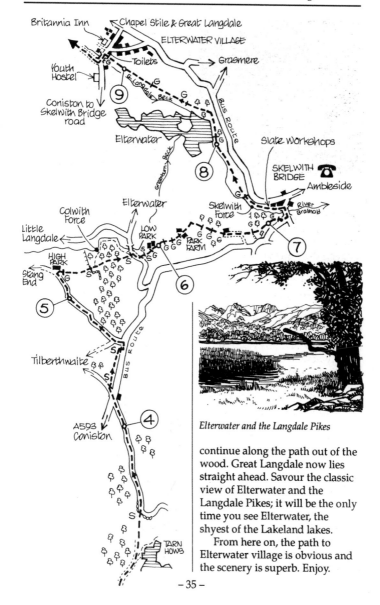

Elterwater and the Langdale Pikes

continue along the path out of the wood. Great Langdale now lies straight ahead. Savour the classic view of Elterwater and the Langdale Pikes; it will be the only time you see Elterwater, the shyest of the Lakeland lakes.

From here on, the path to Elterwater village is obvious and the scenery is superb. Enjoy.

Elterwater village green

A refreshment stop at the Brittania Inn, Elterwater is highly recommended. The village, almost Walt Disney twee now, with a pretty pub, a tumbling beck, slate cottages, a sycamore tree on the green and a shop on the corner, was once an important industrial centre, producing most of Britain's gunpowder needs in a large factory behind the pub.

Suitably fortified, cross the stone bridge over the river and immediately turn right up the lane on the other bank to climb through attractive, birch

Wainwrights Inn

woodland. Where the lane levels out, you can look down into the controversial Langdale timeshare estate, opened in 1981 on the old gunpowder factory site.

Soon you arrive at heaps of slate debris from the quarries higher up. Follow the path down a slate hill to the river bank. Turn upstream for 200 yards and cross a footbridge at Wainwrights Inn onto the road.

Turn left along the roadside for about 200 yards, then take a path on your left just before a walled wood on the outskirts of the small village of Chapel Stile.

Follow the path round to Thrang Farm and an amazing view of the Langdale Pikes framed between a rock restriction in the valley. Continue past the farmhouse into a narrow walled pathway. This swings left beneath slate crags to cross a stone bridge over the river into a peaceful meadow.

The way ahead crosses flat

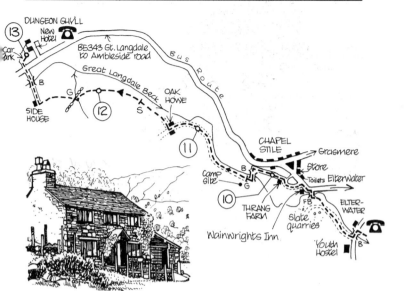

Oak Howe

fields along the raised river bank,
fortified by boulders against the
frightening flash floods which can
sweep down the valley after
heavy rain on the dalehead fells.

After about a mile, the track
swings left into rougher country,
broken by bracken and rocks. At
the lonely outpost of Oak Howe,
turn sharp right and follow the
path beside a broken-down stone
wall. You may have to splash
through mud and small becks
along here.

The path climbs easily across
the fellside, curving gently left
until quite suddenly the Langdale
Pikes appear in all their rugged
glory. What a splendid sight to

end a wonderful day's walking!

The path now descends gently
to Side House. Turn right in the
farmyard and cross the flat valley
floor to Dungeon Ghyll.

Side House

WALK RECORD

Section 2 - Coniston to Dungeon Ghyll – 13 miles

Date walked

25 - 2 . 03

Departure time from Coniston	Arrival time at Dungeon Ghyll
9 . 30	3 . 00

Weather conditions

FINE, DRY SUNNY

Notes

STAYING @ D.D.G.

Poor Food & Service

Never STAY Here AGAIN

CAR PARK   PACK PARK   TRAVELLERS REST

Dungeon Ghyll

Dungeon Ghyll is the most rural of the Cumbria Way stopovers. Don't expect shops or sparkling nightlife. The bars can be pretty lively of a balmy summer's evening, but the best entertainment here is definitely of the outdoor variety. And that's not just on the camp site! Here the scenery is the thing. It's plentiful. It never closes. It's ever-changing and it's free! Enjoy.

Pavey Ark and Stickle Tarn

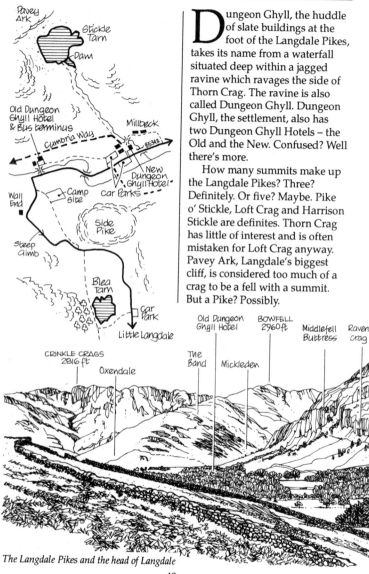

D ungeon Ghyll, the huddle of slate buildings at the foot of the Langdale Pikes, takes its name from a waterfall situated deep within a jagged ravine which ravages the side of Thorn Crag. The ravine is also called Dungeon Ghyll. Dungeon Ghyll, the settlement, also has two Dungeon Ghyll Hotels – the Old and the New. Confused? Well there's more.

How many summits make up the Langdale Pikes? Three? Definitely. Or five? Maybe. Pike o' Stickle, Loft Crag and Harrison Stickle are definites. Thorn Crag has little of interest and is often mistaken for Loft Crag anyway. Pavey Ark, Langdale's biggest cliff, is considered too much of a crag to be a fell with a summit. But a Pike? Possibly.

The Langdale Pikes and the head of Langdale

Even the Pikes themselves, dominating the scene like two majestic sleeping lions, are not all they might seem. All will be revealed at Stake Pass summit.

Above the Pikes, a descending shoulder of Bowfell known as The Band divides upper Langdale into two distinct sections; Mickleden, which stretches two further miles northwards with little change of elevation, and Oxendale, the steeply rising walker's route to Crinkle Crags and Bowfell.

The valley road hairpins sharply out of Oxendale to Blea Tarn, most photogenic of the Lakeland tarns, especially when

seen against the rugged Pikes. All three (or five) of the famous trio (or quintet) of summits can be seen from the tarn. Pike o' Stickle, not in sight from Dungeon Ghyll, and perversely, as seems the fashion here, the one furthest away from Stickle Tarn, soars in a single impressive leap to a tapering thimble of rock at the top.

Particularly hard slivers of rock found on the Pike o' Stickle scree slope have been identified as prehistoric stone axes. A man-made cave discovered high on the pike convinced experts that this was once one of the country's most important axe-making sites.

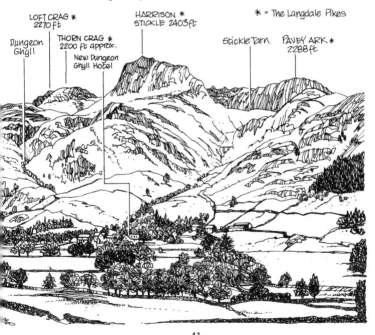

LOFT CRAG *
2270 ft

HARRISON *
STICKLE 2403 ft

* = The Langdale Pikes

Dungeon Ghyll

THORN CRAG *
2200 ft approx.

New Dungeon Ghyll Hotel

Stickle Tarn

PAVEY ARK *
2288 ft

WHAT TO SEE

Stickle Tarn and Pavey Ark

A lovely lakeland tarn with a beach, set beneath the awesome, crumbling rock face of Pavey Ark.

Jake's Rake, a narrow ledge path rising diagonally across the cliff face, should only be attempted by rock climbers.

The path up the gill to Stickle Tarn is one of the most popular in Lakeland. A pleasant evening stroll, steep in places, but well worth the effort for the dramatic scenery.

Blea Tarn

An alternative evening excursion. Take the path across the valley and climb up the other side. A narrow unfenced road passes the low-lying tarn. A Lakeland icon.

Breath-taking in autumn colours.

GETTING THERE

Bus – Summer service from Ambleside.
Enquiries tel: (01946) 63222
Road – **A593** & **B5343** from Ambleside.
A593 & **B5343** from Coniston.

CAMP SITES

National Trust Site, Great Langdale.
Tel: (015394) 37668

Field site at Baysbrown Farm, Chapel Stile. Tel: (015394) 37300

TOURIST INFORMATION

The Old Court House,
Church Street, Ambleside.
Tel: (015394) 32582

WHERE TO STAY

New Dungeon Ghyll Hotel,
Great Langdale.
Tel: (015394) 37213

Old Dungeon Ghyll Hotel,
Great Langdale.
Tel: (015394) 37272

Britannia Inn, Elterwater.
Tel: (015394) 37210

Baysbrown Farm, Chapel Stile.
Tel: (015394) 37300

Long House, Great Langdale.
Tel: (015394) 37222

Stonethwaite, Elterwater.
Tel: (015394) 37244

Greenbank, Skelwith Bridge.
Tel: (015394) 33236

Note - This is not a recommended list. Always phone ahead with your own requirements.

WHERE TO EAT

Old Dungeon Ghyll Hotel.
Tel: (015394) 37272
Walker's Bar food (big helpings!). Last orders 8.30pm. Served in old cowshed. Highly recommended.

New Dungeon Ghyll Hotel.
Tel: (015394) 37213. Climber's Bar.

YOUTH HOSTEL

Elterwater.
Tel: (015394) 41323

3

Dungeon Ghyll to Keswick
16 miles

MAPS

English Lakes 1:25 000 South West and North West sheets.
Or OS Landranger 1:50 000. Sheet 90.

REFRESHMENTS

Elterwater: Britannia Inn. Village shop.
Chapel Stile: Wainwrights Inn. Village store.

BAD WEATHER GET-OUTS

Coniston to Skelwith Bridge: Coniston to Ambleside buses.
Skelwith Bridge to Dungeon Ghyll: Road to Ambleside always close, but you might have a long wait for a bus.

WHAT IS IT LIKE?

Arguably the best section on the Cumbria Way. Easy start into the vast rock cathedral of Mickleden, then a sharp, steep climb over Stake Pass into the wild Langstrath valley. Lush Borrowdale is a wonderful contrast.

BEST BIT

Can't pick. It's superb overall.

Fellside path behind the Old Hotel

Go through the gates behind the New Hotel on the Stickle Tarn track. As soon as you are on the fell, turn left along a path behind the stone wall. Climb up the hill and go through a gate onto a well-worn path running across the foot of the Pikes.

Half a mile on, set amongst trees on your left, stands the Old Hotel, over 300 years old, and one of the most famous mountaineers' and walkers' hostelries in the country. Raven Crag, the great slab of rock behind the hotel, attracts rock climbers from near and far, eager to prove their salt.

Beyond the Old Hotel, the path widens to a track and swings right into Mickleden, the final leg of the long 'S'-shaped Great Langdale valley. Ringed on three sides by high steep mountains, there seems to be no way out, but have no fear!

When carving out Mickleden the melting glaciers paused at the top end and left behind a series of moraines, which now look like enormous mole hills scattered across the otherwise flat valley floor.

At a marking stone, fork right and zig-zag up Stake Pass. A pack horse route for centuries, the pass became seriously eroded by the more recent tramping of walking boots, but has been sensitively repaired by building a natural rock pavement to walk on. Please respect the area and do not stray. The destructive effect of boot erosion can be clearly seen across the valley in Rossett Gill.

The pass climbs to a grassy plateau and wanders unsurely around more moraines and patches of swampy ground. This is a significant watershed. All the water seen on the walk so far eventually flows into Morecambe Bay to the south. From now on the water flows north or west to join the Solway Firth.

Cairn at the foot of Stake Pass

Mickleden from Stake Pass summit

Around the edges of the plateau, the summits of the mighty Langdale Pikes poke lamely above the drab moorland. Seen from here they look very ordinary nobbles of rock. The summit of Pike o' Stickle stands barely 200 feet above the grass. What a let-down.

So, what you see of the Pikes from the valley floor is more or less what you get. But what you do get is considerable.

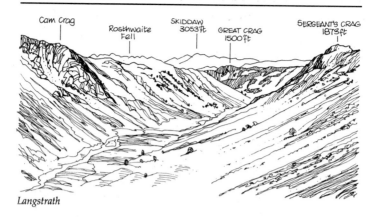

Langstrath

Langstrath is one of the bleakest and stoniest of Lakeland valleys, almost treeless and with little on the smooth fell sides to excite the walker's eyes.

The descent from Stake Pass summit into Langstrath, however, is a delight, fairly steep, zig-zagging down 500 feet in less than a quarter mile alongside Langstrath

The head of Langstrath

Beck, rated by the painter, W. Heaton Cooper, 'the wildest, rockiest, most colourful and interesting mountain stream in England'.

Again, erosion is a problem and parts of the beckside have been fenced off to promote regrowth. Please do as the notices ask. One reads like a Stephen King novel; 'Water will follow your footprints and can cause massive washouts'.

At the foot of the descent, keep to the right-hand side of the valley, along a rough and stoney track which meanders wearily through a wasteland of weathered blocks of stone.

After about two miles, there's relief for the feet when the path joins Greenup Gill, the pack horse route over to Grasmere. Here the Cumbria Way turns abruptly left into Borrowdale.

This corner is a good place to stop for while. Have a look at the beck, foaming and slithering across a series of steps carved into the world's hardest slate, Borrowdale volcanic. The deep pools below the steps are popular, if cold, bathing places for hardy swimmers from the camp site further downstream.

Above the bend in the river looms Eagle Crag, a great bastion of rock forming the cornerstone between Langstrath and Greenup Gill, and renowned as one of major tests in Borrowdale for the hard men of rock climbing.

One of the routes on the crag, graded 'extreme,' is called, in the gallows humour of mountain men, *Post Mortem*. Nuff said.

A lonely Langstrath tree

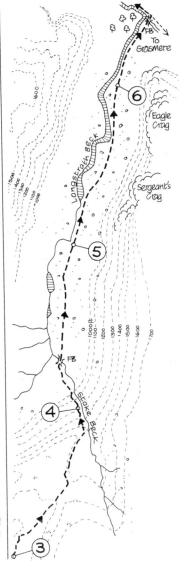

SERGEANT'S CRAG
1873 ft

Eagle Crag

Continue along the rough track down the right hand side of the river. The substantial wooden contraptions across the becks flowing down the deep gulleys on your right are designed to prevent rock debris brought down by flood water blocking up the main river.

If you want to camp at Stonethwaite Farm, cross the river at the first footbridge you come to. For Chapel House Farm camp site or Longthwaite Youth Hostel, cross Stonethwaite Bridge over the river and turn right along the lane. Chapel House Farm site is in the first field left when you come to the main road. For the Youth Hostel, go straight across the main road into another lane, cross the bridge over the river, then turn left along the western bank.

The Cumbria Way continues along the eastern side of Stonethwaite Beck to Rosthwaite. As you progress downstream, upper Borrowdale is gradually revealed, looking ultra-green and lush after barren Stonethwaite.

Stonethwaite Bridge

There should be no problem with the route – just follow the obvious path, and probably the crowds. A popular round walk from Rosthwaite goes up one side of the river to Greenup Gill for a picnic, then returns down the other side. Great for kids.

Cross the stone bridge at Rosthwaite and turn left for the well-stocked village store and post office.

Rosthwaite, sheltered from the winter winds by a low, tree-topped crag, straddles Borrowdale unobtrusively. Slate buildings stand on the ground their walls were cut from, in perfect harmony with their surroundings. Wisps of smoke rising from a dozen chimneys only adds to the appeal of this most romantic of Lakeland valleys.

North of Rosthwaite, the valley narrows and appears to be blocked by Castle Crag, the core of an ancient volcano rising above the trees, a golden tooth perfectly set in the Jaws of Borrowdale.

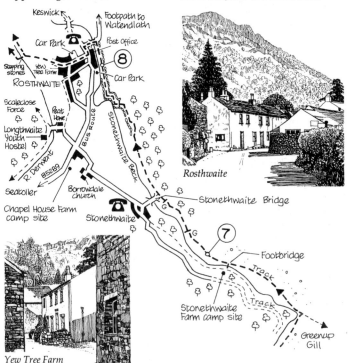

Rosthwaite

Yew Tree Farm

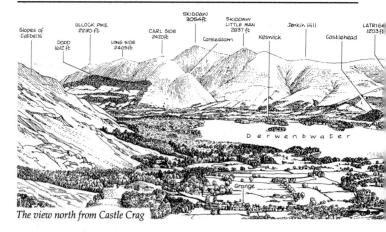

Slopes of Cat bells
DODD 1612 ft
ULLOCK PIKE 2230 ft
LONG SIDE 2405 ft
CARL SIDE 2420 ft
SKIDDAW 3054 ft
Carsleddam
SKIDDAW LITTLE MAN 2837 ft
Keswick
Jenkin Hill
Castlehead
LATRIGG 1203 ft

D e r w e n t w a t e r

Grange

The view north from Castle Crag

Go down the lane opposite the post office to the river. Cross by the stepping stones or continue along the eastern bank to New Bridge and cross.

The official Cumbria Way continues along the river bank and through High Hows Wood to Gowder Dub. When sunlight dapples the silver birches and moss-covered boulders it's a delight every step of the way.

Rosthwaite Post Office

Great archways of ancient oak and beech trees dip to the clearest water and the most beautifully coloured pebble river bed you'll ever find outside of a garden centre showroom. It's like a stroll through a romantic painting. Honest. In his *Guide to the North Western Fells*, Wainwright called this area 'the loveliest square mile in Lakeland'. Few people would disagree.

Wonderful though the river bank route is, you do miss out on the tremendous views from the top of Castle Crag. The crag is only about 985 feet high, so climbing it is not going to finish you off for the rest of the day. Anyway, the adrenaline rush you will get from the short climb and the breath-taking views from the top will last you well into Keswick and beyond. In fine weather, the short diversion is far too good to miss.

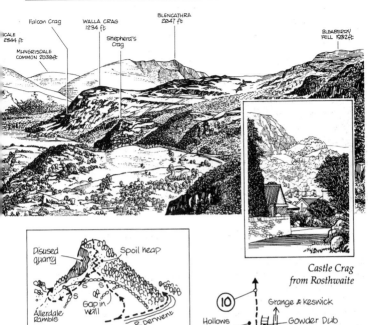

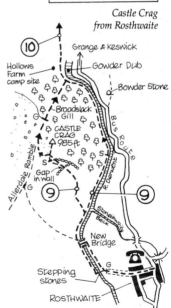

Falcon Crag

WALLA CRAG
1234 ft

BLENCATHRA
2847 ft

SCALE
2844 ft

Shepherd's
Crag

BLEABERRY
FELL 1932ft

MUNGRISDALE
COMMON 2038ft

*Castle Crag
from Rosthwaite*

Disused
quarry

Spoil heap

Allerdale
Ramble

Gap in
wall

R. Derwent

An ascent of Castle Crag

After crossing New Bridge, take the path on your left, climbing up the field towards Castle Crag. A stile at the top takes you onto the crag itself, where an obvious path zig-zags in little steps up a slate spoil heap. The final section onto the flat, grassy top is clear ahead. Careful going past the old mine workings.

Descend by the slate stairway, turning right at the bottom to cross a couple of stiles onto a rough track. Turn right down Broadslack Gill and go through Low Hows wood to rejoin the official Cumbria Way at Gowder Dub.

⑩ Grange & Keswick

Hollows
Farm
camp site

Gowder Dub

Bowder Stone

Broadslack
Gill

CASTLE
CRAG
985ft

Allerdale Ramble

Gap
in wall

R. Derwent

Bus Route

⑨ ⑨

Stonethwaite
Beck

New
Bridge

Stepping
stones

ROSTHWAITE

Gowder Dub on the River Derwent

Keep on the track along the river bank. Camping in the wood and adjoining field is managed by Hollows Farm.

The official Cumbria Way turns left at the end of the wood, going up the lane past Hollows Farm and along the fell bottom. Unfortunately, this route misses out the delightful lakeland hamlet of Grange.

The tiny settlement is always worth a visit, if only for a cup of coffee or to use the public toilets. To go to Grange, bear right along the lane at the end of the wood.

A significant geological change in the underlying rock can clearly be seen on the fell above Hollows Farm. The craggy fells to the south are hard Borrowdale Volcanic slate, which splits well for roofing purposes. The more smooth-sided fells to the north are of the softer Skiddaw slate, one of the oldest rocks in Europe, which shatters into small pieces, useless for building.

Grange-in-Borrowdale was established in the 14th century by Furness Abbey monks as the administration centre for their considerable business affairs in the valley. None of the original settlement remains though some of the cottages are reputed to have walls of monastic stone. Spiritual matters are still well taken care of by the tiny 1894 methodist church and the handsome Holy Trinity church, built of local slate in 1860.

Looking south from Grange

Grange Farm, at the end of the central green, was model for the house of Roque Herries in the quartet of Lakeland novels by Hugh Walpole. He lived a mile up the road at Brackenburn.

The best known feature of Grange is the double arched bridge, built of local slate in 1675 to span the broad River Derwent. Multitudes of summer visitors picnic by the bridge and bathe in the remarkably clear river.

Return to the official Cumbria Way by walking up the road past the church. Keep on the road until about a quarter of a mile past the Borrowdale Gates Hotel. Here, just beyond Ellers Beck, take the signposted track on your right across a field. This swings left around a wood onto the grassy flood plain at the head of Derwentwater.

Bear left around the bay, using the series of raised wooden walkways if the lake is high, and follow the obvious path into Manesty Park Wood.

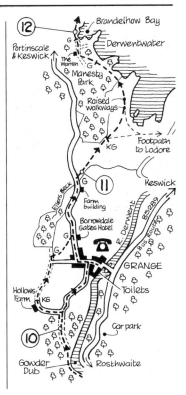

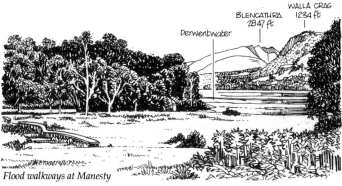

Flood walkways at Manesty

In the wood, you will soon come to a cottage alongside a metalled track. Turn right along the track, through a gateway. Beyond another building, you emerge from the wood onto the stony shore of Brandelhow Bay.

You can now follow the lake shore north around the bays and promontories with terrific views of Skiddaw and Blencathra, or use a straighter path which keeps to the wood a short way inland. In good weather the shore path is the best by far. If it's raining, you might prefer the more sheltered route through the wood.

Brandelhow Wood, a mature mix of mainly beech and oak trees, was the first acquisition in Lakeland by the fledgling National Trust. Canon Rawsley, vicar of Crosthwaite and one of the three founders of the Trust, raised the necessary £6,500 – a tidy sum in 1902 – in only five months.

The route goes past four of the Derwentwater launches' landing stages. There are a further three

Adventure Centre

stopping places along the eastern shore. Two of the launches, built of Burma Teak, originally for the exclusive use of Lodore Hotel patrons, have been in regular service for over 80 years.

Just beyond the Low Brandelhow landing stage, the path turns away from the lake into a field. Keep straight on through a metal kissing gate, then turn right onto a metalled road skirting Hawse End outdoor pursuits centre.

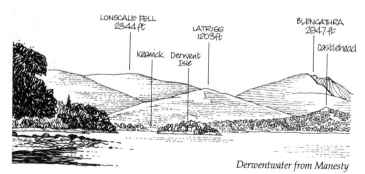

Derwentwater from Manesty

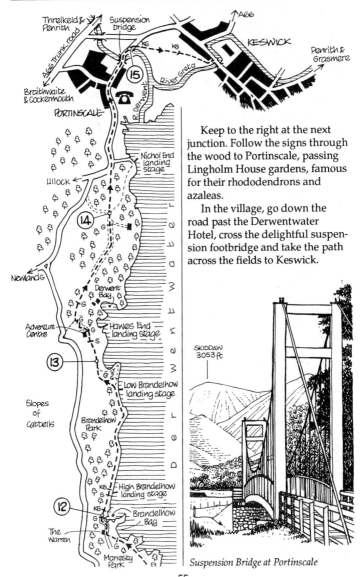

Keep to the right at the next junction. Follow the signs through the wood to Portinscale, passing Lingholm House gardens, famous for their rhododendrons and azaleas.

In the village, go down the road past the Derwentwater Hotel, cross the delightful suspension footbridge and take the path across the fields to Keswick.

Suspension Bridge at Portinscale

WALK RECORD

Section 3 - Dungeon Ghyll to Keswick – 16 miles

Date walked

26. 02. 03

Departure time from Dungeon Ghyll	Arrival time at Keswick
9.00	3.45

Weather conditions

FINE & DRY

Notes

STOPPED @ ROSTHWAITE & GRANGE

STAYING @ RAVENSWORTH HOTEL

V. GOOD ROOM / FAC.

NEW INSOLES, PETE ?

Main street, Keswick

Fabulously set between Derwentwater and Skiddaw, Keswick will always come second best to its surroundings.

The town developed with the local mining industry. In 1564, a decree by Elizabeth the First brought miners from Germany to dig for copper ore in Newlands and Borrowdale. A large smelter, built at Brigham where the A66 road bridge now crosses the Greta, brought a century of prosperity. Then, during the Civil War in 1564, Cromwell's troops destroyed the smelter and with it the Keswick copper industry.

Miners now turned to 'Wad' mines at the head of Borrowdale producing graphite, then a valuable resource with both military and medicinal uses. Locally, it was made into pencils, an industry still carried on in the town. Rexel's high-tech factory now produces nearly half a million pencils a day.

Generated by extravagant writers and the Lake Poets, tourism gradually grew during the nineteenth century. When the railway arrived in 1864, the flood gates opened. Keswick now has more B&Bs than any town of its size anywhere in the country. The railway line closed in 1972 and

Pack Horse Yard

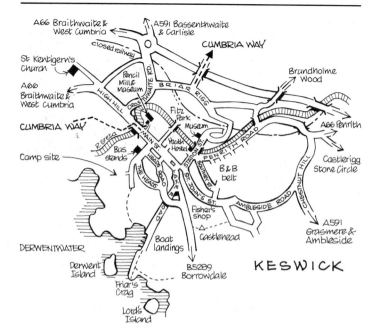

the Keswick Spa opened on the station site in 1987.

The town centre buildings are a hotch-potch of Victoriana with modern shop fronts, but the 1990 development of the Pack Horse Yard and Royal Oak Hotel was more sensitively done.

Keswick's most distinctive building is the Moot Hall in Market Place, though even that dates from 1813. It's been used as a court house, market, prison, museum and town hall. Since 1971, the ground floor has been a tourist information bureau, the busiest in Lakeland with 190,000 visitors a year. On Saturdays,

traffic is banned from Market Place for the market.

Keswick is a perfect walking centre and every street seems to have an outdoor equipment shop. George Fisher's in Lake Road sells everything you'd ever need. There's also an excellent tea room on the top floor where the pioneering mountain photographers, the Abraham brothers, once had their studio.

The Lake Poets, Coleridge and Southey lived at Greta Hall, a handsome three-storey Georgian house overlooking the town.

Another local worthy, the vicar of Crosthwaite, Hardwicke

Drummond Rawnsley, a life-long activist for nature conservation, became one of the three founders of the National Trust in 1893. Rawnsley was also a prolific author and keen educationist. He encouraged the young Beatrix Potter to write.

The Keswick Convention, an international spiritual campaign, was founded in 1875 by the vicar of St John's church and a Quaker friend. Two hundred people attended. Now thousands of pilgrims pack the town annually for two weeks in July. Services are held in a huge marquee erected behind the Convention Centre in Skiddaw Street.

Dorothy and William Wordsworth stayed at Old Windebrowe on the lower slopes of Latrigg to nurse a dying friend, Raisley Calvert, in 1794. He left Wordsworth £900 which enabled him to become a poet.

A stroll down to the lake onto Friar's Crag is obligatory. John Ruskin, who visited when a child

Lake Road

and was suitably impressed, has a monument on the viewpoint.

Amongst the odd collection of curios in the museum and art gallery beside Fitz Park are musical stones from Skiddaw, Turner paintings donated by an American, and documents connected with the Lake Poets and Ruskin. Also Hugh Walpole's handwritten manuscripts. Don't miss the kiddies' favourite, a 500-year old mummified cat – late of Borrowdale.

High Hill

WHAT TO SEE

St Kentigern's Church Crosthwaite. Founded AD553, rebuilt in the 12th century. The poet Southey and National Trust co-founder, Rawnsley, are buried in the churchyard.
George Fisher Borrowdale Road. Tel: (017687) 72178
Blue Box Theatre Lake Road. Tel: (017687) 74411
Live repertory at the lakeside.
Keswick Museum Station Road. Tel: (017687) 73263
Open: Apr-Oct, Mon-Fri 10.00-4.00
Cumberland Pencil Museum Southy Works. Tel: (017687) 73626
Open: Every day, 9.30-4.00.
Derwentwater Launches Boat landings, Lake Road.
Friar's Crag Superb lakeside viewpoint. Just keep on walking past the boat landings.
Castlehead Tree-covered hill, south of St.John's church. Easy climb. The best low-level viewpoint in the Lakes.

GETTING THERE

Bus – Excellent *Lakeslink* service from Kendal via Windermere and Ambleside. Not so good from Penrith or West Cumbria.
Enquiries tel: (01946) 63222
Road – **M6 motorway** junc 40 Penrith onto **A66**.
M6 junc 36 Kendal onto **A591** through Windermere and Ambleside.
A66 from West Cumbria.
A595 and **A591** from Carlisle.

TOURIST INFORMATION

Moot Hall, Market Place.
Tel: (017687) 72645

WHERE TO STAY

Avondale, 20 Southey Street.
Tel: (017687) 72735. Recommended.

Sandon, 13 Southey Street.
Tel: (017687) 73648. Recommended.

Keswick has the highest concentration of B&Bs and guest houses in the country so, provided you avoid the school holidays, you should have no problems finding somewhere to stay – even on spec. Trawl the area bounded by Southey Street, Ambleside Road and Penrith Road. Tourist Information will find and book accommodation within a four weeks period before your arrival date. Dial direct on (01768) 74101

WHERE TO EAT

Plenty to pick from. The Rembrant in Station Street is good value and Bryson's tea room is worth a visit. Some good pub grub, especially The Dog and Gun and The Oddfellows in Market Place.

CAMP SITES

Derwentwater Caravan Park, Crowe Park Road, Keswick.
Tel: (017687) 72579

Walker Park Caravan Park, Keswick.
Tel: (017687) 73607

Lakeside Holiday Park, Keswick.
Tel: (017687) 72878

YOUTH HOSTEL

Station Road, Keswick.
Tel: (017687) 72484

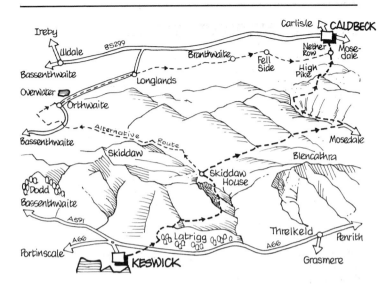

4

Keswick to Caldbeck

16 miles – High Pike route.
18.5 miles – Orthwaite route.

MAPS

English Lakes 1:25 000 North West sheet.
Or OS Landranger 1:50 000 Sheet 90.

REFRESHMENTS

No places to buy food or drink but plenty of good becks for filling-up water bottles.

BEST BIT

Keswick to Skiddaw House.

BAD WEATHER GET-OUTS

Service road from Skiddaw House to Bassenthwaite or Blencathra Centre. Bus service from Threlkeld. Road down the valley to Mosedale from the bottom of Grainsgill. No public transport from Mosedale.

WHAT IS IT LIKE?

An easy climb up Latrigg is followed by a stroll amongst magnificent scenery to Skiddaw House. Then a flat moorland path leads to a soggy climb up Grainsgill to High Pike. There's a gentle, grassy descent to Nether Row and quiet lanes into Caldbeck. Waymarking is almost non-existent, though hardly needed. Alternative bad weather route through Orthwaite is mainly on quiet farm roads. No problems. No steep climbs or descents on either route.

This section starts in the north western corner of Upper Fitz Park. Walk out of the park along the tarred pathway and turn right up the road at the end. Climb the hill past a small housing estate and turn left down a rough track known as Spooney Green Lane.

Once a favourite walk for courting couples, the lane now crosses the noisy and intrusive A66 Keswick by-pass. Stop and mourn the loss of solitude, but also remember the benefits brought to Keswick, and the villages of Portinscale, Braithwaite and Threlkeld, which no longer have to endure a daily battering from heavy traffic.

At the foot of Latrigg, the lane becomes a bridle path and climbs steeply through the trees. A great view of Keswick and the lake appears, then the route curves right, into a fold of Latrigg.

Over a beck, there's more gentle climbing across an open section with a magnificent view of Skiddaw ahead. A final stretch past a dense conifer plantation brings you to Gale Road, a rough track used as an access road for vehicles to Latrigg and Skiddaw.

Turn right and walk up Gale Road to the car park at the top. A kissing gate in the right hand corner opens onto the smooth, grassy flank of Latrigg. It's only a short climb to Latrigg summit, where on a clear day you'll see one of the best views in Lakeland.

No cairn marks the top of Latrigg. There's no rocks to build

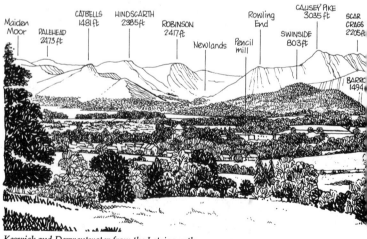

Keswick and Derwentwater from the Latrigg path

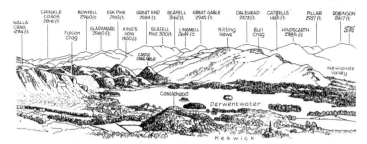

The view south from Latrigg summit

one. All is grass, layered into terracing so you can sit and admire the view. Watch cars cruise round Keswick looking for somewhere to park. See launches slice arrowheads across the lake. Marvel at the endless variety of colours in the trees, and of course, the superb array of fells – the Scafells, Great Gable, the Langdale biggies. And, away in the South and first seen from Gawthwaite on day one of this walk, our old friend Dow Crag.

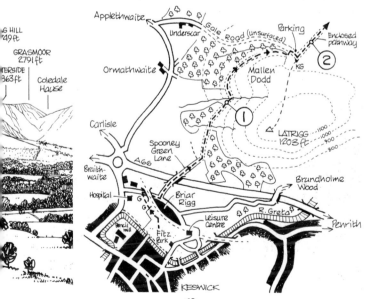

Return to the car park at the top of Gale Road and take the enclosed path across the gently rising back of Latrigg to the foot of Skiddaw. Turn off the Skiddaw path onto a track. This crosses Whit Beck, then contours across the heather-covered side of Lonscale Fell. Blencathra looms ahead and there's good views across Threlkeld to Clough Head.

Suddenly, all changes when the route turns sharp left and you find yourself on a path half way up the steep sided valley of the Glenderaterra Beck. Lonscale Crags rear above. Ahead, the first folds of the grassy nothingness of Skiddaw Forest beckon.

Across the beck, the soft side of Blencathra is gradually revealed. Seen from the south, the mountain is all deep, dramatic ravines and soaring ridges, an awesome sight, irresistible to any

Whit Gill

Path below Lonscale Crags

fellwalker. The north side of Blencathra, however, is nicely rounded and grassy, and of little interest to anyone except sheep.

After a couple of miles, Lonscale Fell drops away and the north side of Skiddaw comes into view away on your left. Like Blencathra and the Langdale Pikes, Skiddaw puts all its best bits on show in the front window and ignores visitors who go nosing about the back door. These acres of open grassland attract few customers to slog up Skiddaw from the north.

Amazingly, this vast area is still called Skiddaw Forest, even though the only trees to be seen these days are the conifers planted as a windbreak for Skiddaw House, a row of four shepherd's cottages which have recently been used as a lonely and spartan Youth Hostel.

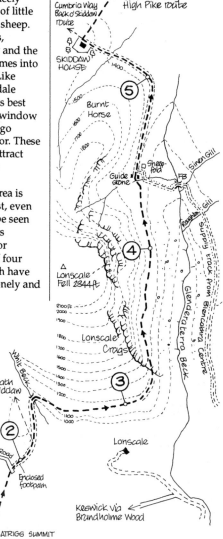

Skiddaw House

The main Cumbria Way turns up the broad valley overlooked by Skiddaw House, then climbs 1500 feet to the summit of High Pike. If mist covers the fell tops when you are at Skiddaw House, the alternative low level route through Orthwaite to Caldbeck is recommended. Turn to page 70 for a description or if you want to visit Bassenthwaite.

Follow the path by the wall down from Skiddaw House, then find the bridge over the infant River Caldew amongst the lush heather. The path keeps to the

river, growing to a broad track in the three miles before the bridge over Grainsgill Beck. Here, the track joins a tarred road and turns down the valley to the hamlet of Mosedale.

Cumbria Way walkers now face a steep climb up Grainsgill to Lingy Hut, which can be seen on the skyline from the bridge

Head up the gill on a metalled track to the ruins of Carrock Mine. Wolfram, a rare heavy metal, was once dug here. Old mines are always dangerous, so KEEP TO THE TRACK. Follow the beck up the gill, a lovely climb, even though the path is indistinct and boggy

Grainsgill

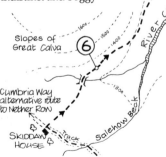

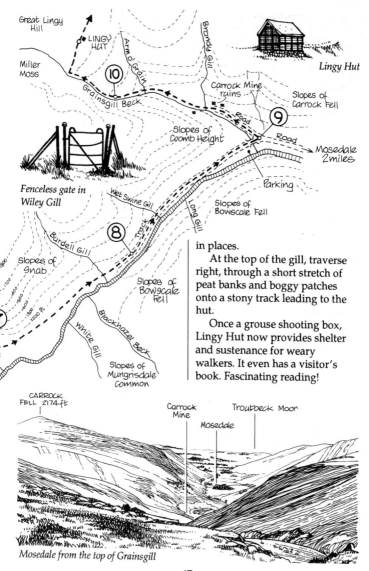

Great Lingy Hill

LINGY HUT

Miller Moss

Arm o' Grain

Brandy Gill

Grainsgill Beck

⑩

Carrock Mine ruins

Road

Slopes of Carrock Fell

Lingy Hut

⑨

Slopes of Coomb Height

Road

Mosedale 2 miles

Fenceless gate in Wiley Gill

Wet Swine Gill

Parking

Slopes of Bowscale Fell

⑧

Long Gill

Burdell Gill

Slopes of Snab

1800 1700 1600 1500 1400 1300 1200 ft

White Gill

Slopes of Bowscale Fell

Blackhazel Beck

Slopes of Mungrisdale Common

Fenceless gate in Wiley Gill

in places.

At the top of the gill, traverse right, through a short stretch of peat banks and boggy patches onto a stony track leading to the hut.

Once a grouse shooting box, Lingy Hut now provides shelter and sustenance for weary walkers. It even has a visitor's book. Fascinating reading!

CARROCK FELL 2174 ft

Carrock Mine

Troutbeck Moor

Mosedale

Mosedale from the top of Grainsgill

High Pike

Keep on the clear track beyond the hut for about a mile. When it sweeps right, leave the track and head up the rough grass slope on your left to High Pike summit, the highest point on the Cumbria Way.

At 2157 feet the top is not particularly high, nor does it have any kind of rocky outcrop which could justify the 'pike' tag. It is, however, the most northerly Lakeland summit over 2000 feet, and commands an extensive view northwards across the Solway Firth to the Scottish hills and eastwards across the broad Eden Valley to the lumpy Pennines.

Heaps of stones litter the summit itself like an abandoned building site. Some stones have been gathered together to make a rough cairn and a shelter. Others have been built into an OS triangulation column. Yet more make a beacon. Just north of the summit are the stone ruins of a shepherd's cottage. Even more surprising amongst this scene of desolation is the presence of a highly polished slate seat. This replaced an ornamental garden seat that sheep kept getting their horns stuck in.

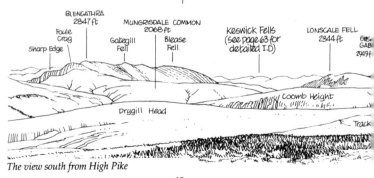

The view south from High Pike

The seat commemorates Mick Lewis of Nether Row, who died, aged 16, in 1944. A plaque says he 'loved all these fells'. A sentiment easy to empathize with after four days on the Cumbria Way.

The simplest way down to the Nether Row lane is to just walk down the grassy fellside, taking care to avoid the old mine workings. In bad weather, return to the track from Lingy Hut and follow it north to join the track into Nether Row at the cleared site of the Potts Gill Mine buildings. An aerial ropeway used to carry buckets of ore from here to Nether Row. You'll have to walk. Much pleasanter.

High Pike summit

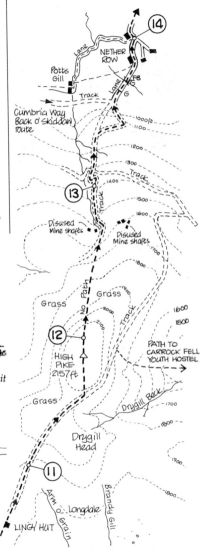

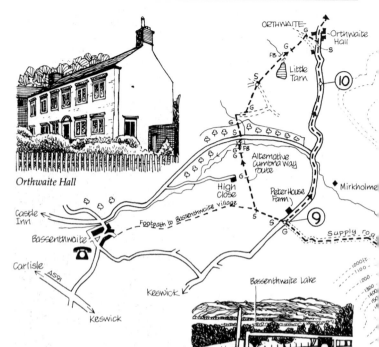

Orthwaite Hall

Stile near Peter House Farm

Continue northwards beyond Skiddaw House on the track once trod only by shepherds. Pearson Dalton of Fellside use to live during the week at Skiddaw House with only his dogs for company. He did it for nearly 50 years until his retirement at the age of 75 in 1969. Fans call this vast open area 'Back o' Skidda'. Others, happier in a more refined environment perhaps, might call it the 'Back o' Beyond'.

Even Dash Beck seems glad to escape the wilderness, plunging down Whitewater Dash in an exuberant series of roaring cataracts as soon as the green fields of Bassenthwaite come into sight. Dead Crags rear dramatically over the falls, the last flourish northwards of the mighty Skiddaw massif.

The track joins the road near Peter House Farm. From here you can simply walk along the quiet road to Orthwaite, or you can take the fields route, descending to cross Dash Beck, then climbing past Little Tarn to Orthwaite.

A visit to Bassenthwaite adds another three miles to this already 18.5 miles-long stage, though the village does have an excellent pub and, if you decide to abandon walking for the day, plenty of B&B accommodation.

Orthwaite is little more than a collection of farm buildings strung across the lower slopes of the Uldale Fells. Pretty Orthwaite Hall catches the eye, but the fells are bleak and confusing for walkers. The inexperienced who venture could easily end up lost on aptly-named Great Cockup.

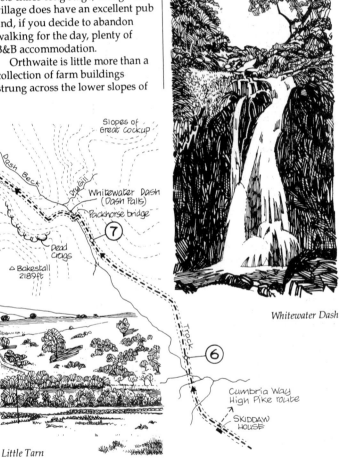

Whitewater Dash

Little Tarn

–71–

Keep going northwards on the narrow road from Orthwaite. After about a mile, you pass Overwater, the only lake in the northern arc of Lakeland. As the slopes of Great Cockup decline on your right, the landscape broadens and, opposite a road going off left to the village of

Overwater

Uldale, the wooded valley of Stockdale opens up. This is the source of the River Ellen, a major watercourse, which flows through Chapel House Reservoir, then meanders around the West Cumbria villages and flows into the Solway Firth at Maryport.

After crossing Longlands Beck, and just before the farming complex of Longlands, go over a stile on your right onto an old highway which passes behind

Low Longlands Farm and a small conifer plantation.

The track continues across the fell bottom, arcing round the foot of Longlands Fell and crossing Charlton Gill onto the lower slopes of Brea Fell. You now descend gently to a couple of farms gathered round a stone bridge at Greenhead.

Go over the bridge and follow the road to the slightly larger farming community of Branthwaite.

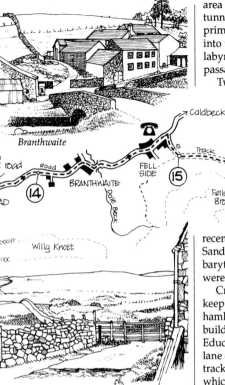

area of Skiddaw slates. The tunnels and shafts, hewn with primitive tools, penetrated deep into the fellsides, forming a labyrinth of underground passages along the mineral veins.

Two mines opened in more

Return to the fell at Longlands

The break in the barrier of fells on your right is Roughton Gill, site of the once renowned but long abandoned Roughtongill Lead Mines. Dating back to the sixteenth century, they were reputed to have yielded 23 different ores and minerals. Once, ten mines scarred the High Pike slopes, all located within a narrow belt of volcanic rock bounding the

recent times, Potts Gill and Sandbed, produced the mineral barytes profitably for a while, but were finally closed in the 1960s.

Cross Branthwaite Beck and keep on the road through the hamlet of Fellside to the last building, Fellside Outdoor Education Centre. Here, turn up a lane on your right onto a rising track, paved with concrete blocks, which crosses the fell bottom.

Keep above Little Fellside Farm and
EITHER follow the track climbing slightly to join the main Cumbria Way at the cleared Potts Gill Mine site,
OR go onto another track at a lower level, keeping above a wall, to a beck near Potts Gill Farm. Follow the beck through the farmyard. Beyond the farm, a clear track ambles across the fields to Nether Row.

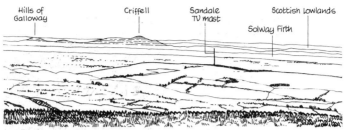

Hills of Galloway · Criffell · Sandale TV mast · Scottish Lowlands · Solway Firth

The view north from High Pike

These days, Nether Row displays little of its industrial background. A handful of pretty cottages gathered round a small green are all that is left. Only the many tracks and lanes leading off give a hint of the busy crossroads that this once was. The main route to Caldbeck village is the green lane straight ahead.

As you walk gently downhill the massive bulk of High Pike becomes more evident behind you and the smooth slopes of the 'Back o' Skiddaw' fells come into view.

This is John Peel country. Here Caldbeck's most famous son hunted the fox from daybreak to sundown, sometimes covering 60 miles a day on horseback. His long-suffering wife, Mary, bore

Clay Bottom Farm

him 13 children, but Peel was no family man. He was killed in a riding accident at the age of 78. Thousands of people turned out for his funeral at Caldbeck.

Peel would have remained only a local character if it hadn't been for John Woodcock Graves, the Wigton-born manager of a Caldbeck woollen factory, who wrote some off-the-cuff words about Peel in 1829 to sing to the tune of the old Scottish lullaby, 'Bonnie Annie'.

A year after writing the lyrics, Graves left his wife to lead the life of a ne'er-do-well in Tasmania. He died there in 1886.

In 1869, 15 years after Peel's death, the choirmaster of Carlisle cathedral, William Metcalf, gave the song a new tune, creating the version of *D'ye Ken John Peel* now sung by damp-eyed Cumbrian exiles all over the world.

Go straight over the crossroads into the lane signed '6'-6" except for access'. After about 200 yards, cross an open area on your right and climb over a stile into a field. Bear left, heading for another stile to the right of a house on the other side of the field.

Cross the narrow lane to a stone stile into another field. Keep to the edge of the field, then climb a stile over a wire fence and go down the hill through the trees to a footbridge over the beck.

On the other side, a narrow fenced path passes some houses, then opens onto a road, only a few yards from the centre of Caldbeck.

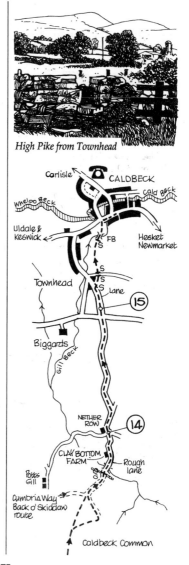

High Pike from Townhead

WALK RECORD

| Section 4 - Keswick to Caldbeck | |
High Pike route – 16 miles	Orthwaite route – 18.5 miles
Date walked 27/2/03	Date walked
Departure time from Keswick 9.10	Departure time from Keswick
Arrival time at Caldbeck 3 15	Arrival time at Caldbeck
Weather conditions FINE- DRY DAY	Weather conditions

Notes ANN LINGHY 1.PM. GOOD CLEAR CONDITIONS - WIND PICKING UP. TOOK SLIGHT WRONG TURN DOWN FROM HIGH PIKE BUE TO ENJOYING VIEWS THANKFULLY ONLY COST US ABOUT ANOTHER ½/1 MILE. STAYED @ ODDFELLOWS BEST FOOD & HOSPITALITY OF THE WEEK BRILLIANT.

Caldbeck village centre

Caldbeck is a large, pretty and prosperous-looking village, with a traditional village green, a duckpond and a big population of ducks. Isolated from tourist Lakeland, it's more a commuter village for Carlisle than a coach party honeypot.

The settlement began as a farming community around the twelfth century Church of St Kentigern's, then mineral wealth was discovered in the local fells and the village grew dramatically. During the nineteenth century, eight mills operated along the river. Corn was ground, wool spun, paper made, bobbins turned. Limestone was quarried, and silver, lead, copper and barytes mined in the vicinity. Coal was dug in the village itself, from shallow pits on Ratten Row. With the industry came the associated cloggers, blacksmiths and, of course, a brewery. In 1827 Caldbeck had seven alehouses.

Digging the ore must have been punishing enough, but the eighteenth century miners also had to carry it across the fells to be smelted at Keswick. A journey comparable to Section 4 of The Cumbria Way in reverse!

St Kentigern's Church and Cald Beck

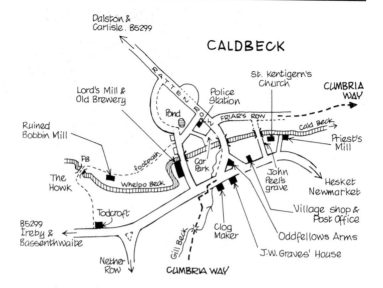

Priest's Mill, down a lane past the church, was built in 1702 by the rector who also built the church tower in 1727. Milling ended in the 1930s.

The building was beautifully restored in 1985 and now houses the superb Watermill Restaurant, a mining museum and shops. The museum charts the history of local mining and displays tools, lamps and specimens.

St Kentigern's is a large, well-maintained church, founded about 1140 on the spot where the saint had preached in 553AD. St Mungo's Well, said to have been used by Kentigern to baptise converts, still gurgles on the river bank behind the church. Basically Norman in style, the building has been much added to and modified over the centuries.

John Peel's grave is well signposted to the left of the church door. More difficult to find is the grave of Mary Harrison, who is better known as the 'Beauty of Buttermere'. She was duped into a bigamous marriage by John Hatfield, masquerading as a nobleman. He was found guilty of forgery in a sensational trial and was hanged at Carlisle in 1803. Mary eventually married a Caldbeck farmer.

The Beauty of Buttermere story has been dramatized several times, most recently in a 1987 novel by Melvyn Bragg, a native of Wigton, who has a house at Ireby, near Caldbeck.

Mountaineers Chris Bonington and Doug Scott also live not far away.

In a wooded dell upstream from Lord's Mill and the old Brewery lies the ruins of the bobbin mill where 60 local men and boys once worked. Power came from an enormous 42ft diameter water wheel, the largest in England at the time. The mill closed about 1920, but the great wheel survived until 1940, when it was scrapped for the war effort.

Nearby, the generally peaceful Whelpo Beck abruptly charges through The Howk, a scooping out of the limestone bed into a spectacular gorge. In two deep holes, The Fairy Kettle and The Fairy Kirk, the water spins and froths with agitation.

The romantic Victorians loved to come here for large organised picnics, outings advertised and reported on in the local paper.

The woollen mill, now a private house, stands where the

Ruined bobbin mill in the Howk

Cumbria Way enters the village. Here, under the management of John Peel's friend, J.W. Graves, grey homespun cloth was produced using undyed Herdwick wool. Peel's coat so 'grey' – not 'gay' as is often sung – was made of it.

An evening stroll round Caldbeck is the perfect way to end a wonderful day's walking.

The Oddfellows Arms and Graves' house

WHAT TO SEE

The Howk Follow the signs from the gate near the duck pond.

Priest's Mill Tel: (016974) 78369 Mining museum, shops & restaurant.

St Kentigern's Church Atmospheric building. Famous churchyard residents.

Caldbeck itself including Upton, up the hill west of the main village. Many houses have been modernised, but Caldbeck remains the least spoilt of the large Lakeland villages.

The Old Crown Hesket Newmarket. Only a mile and a half away from Caldbeck, but worth the walk for the Real Beer, brewed on the premises. Handy if you're staying at the Youth Hostel. Pretty village too.

GETTING THERE

Note Caldbeck has virtually no public transport. However, if you are stuck, the local coach and minibus company, Tyson's of Caldbeck, may be able to help.

Ring them on (016974) 78237

Road – **B5299** from Carlisle or West Cumbria. Minor road via Mungrisdale from **A66** Penrith or Keswick.

YOUTH HOSTEL

Carrock Fell Youth Hostel, High Row Cottages, Haltcliffe. Tel: (016974) 78325

CAMP SITE

No public site in the Caldbeck area.

TOURIST INFORMATION

Priest's Mill. Mainly leaflets for callers.

WHERE TO STAY

The Oddfellows Arms, Caldbeck. Tel: (016974) 78227

Brownrigg Farm, Caldbeck. Tel: (016974) 78268

Friar Hall, Friar's Row, Caldbeck. Tel: (016974) 78633. Recommended.

Height Farm, Caldbeck. Tel: (016974) 78668

Swaledale Watch, Whelpo. Tel: (016974) 78409 Working farm, one mile west of Caldbeck village.

High Greenrigg House. Tel: (016974) 78430 Near Greenhead on Cumbria Way alternative route. Recommended.

Note - This is not a recommended list unless specified. Always phone ahead with your own requirements.

WHERE TO EAT

The Oddfellows Arms, Caldbeck. Tel: (016974) 78227

Priest's Mill, Caldbeck. Tel: (016974) 78369

Parkend Restaurant, Parkend. Tel: (016974) 78494

Old Crown, Hesket Newmarket. Tel: (016974) 78288

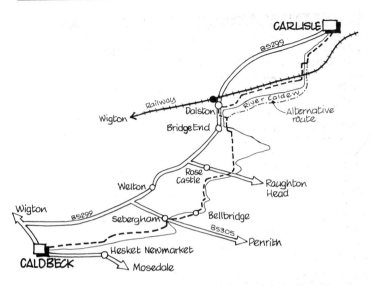

5 Caldbeck to Carlisle 15 miles

MAPS

OS Landranger 1:50 000. Sheet 90
Penrith, Keswick & Ambleside
and Sheet 85 Carlisle &
The Solway Firth.

REFRESHMENTS

Bridge End: Pub.
Dalston: Pubs and shops.

BEST BIT

Bellbridge to Bridge End.

BAD WEATHER GET-OUTS

B5299 road between Caldbeck and
Carlisle runs almost parallel to the
walk route. There's virtually no bus
service between Caldbeck and
Bridge End. From Bridge End to
Carlisle the service is much better.

WHAT IS IT LIKE?

Definitely a winding down section
after the heady delights of the Lake
District. Steady walking on good
paths, initially through woodland and
then across farmland for most of the
way into Carlisle. The River Caldew, a
constant and interesting companion,
causes problems during wet weather
by flooding and in some places
actually washing away the path. This
section is the best waymarked part of
the Cumbria Way.

Wind turbines at Newlands

The final section begins on the lane across the river from St Kentigern's church. Head downstream through a gate. Pass the village sewerage works to the edge of Parson's Park wood. Ignore the stile over the wire fence and go through the gate near the river instead.

After a rather muddy 200 yards along the riverside, there is a junction of paths. The one on the right goes straight ahead between rows of conifers. The bridleway curving away to the left is the route to take. This is an important junction. Make sure you take the branch going left.

After an initially steep section, the track climbs more slowly, then levels out for about half a mile through mixed woodland. Keep to the obviously more worn track you are on and ignore the other overgrown tracks going off.

The track through the wood ends with a short climb to a gate in a wire fence. Beyond is a park-like open stretch for about half a mile. Keep at about the same height across the slope.

You are now high enough to see over the wooded river gorge. The wind turbines, which generate power to make cowcake, can hardly be missed on the hillside at Newlands. High Crag and Blencathra still show prominently to the south west.

Keep topside of a clump of

The 'crucial' point

trees and go through a gate in a wire fence into the next field. Head diagonally across it, climbing gradually to a gate in a stone wall into a plantation.

About 500 yards into the wood, along a typical conifer forest track, the route abruptly turns right and goes down through the wood to the river. This junction can easily be missed, so keep a look out for the crucial point just before a clearing in the trees. Don't worry too much if you do miss it. Just keep on the forest track to the end of the wood where you can rejoin the track into Sebergham.

The main trail follows the river bank. Pick your way over a large landslip. Leave the wood over a stile into a field. Follow the path along the edge of the wood to join a track. This takes you into Sebergham, a hamlet gathered round a stone bridge over the River Caldew.

Cross the bridge and turn left beyond the first house where a sign says 'Public bridleway to Sebergham church'. Go through the metal gate into a field.

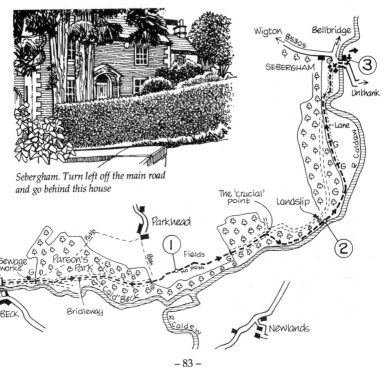

Sebergham. Turn left off the main road and go behind this house

Sebergham church

Follow the grassy track round to the right, keeping close to the wire fence up a short hill. Go through a gate at the top and along a tarmac lane to the church. Turn left down another lane opposite the church marked 'Public bridleway to Bellbridge.'

Go over a cattle grid and through a gate to Sebergham Hall. A sign on the gate says 'Cumbria Way', a rarity on this generally poorly waymarked walk.

Keep to the right of the Hall grounds. The track descends over another cattle grid to the old stone bridge at Bellbridge, where

Lanehead Mill

a signpost give the distance to Carlisle as nine and a quarter miles. How's the blisters?

From here to Rose Bridge the banks of the river are subject to erosion and from time to time there are floods. If you can see water in the fields ahead when you are at Bell Bridge, you are advised to take a diversion. Go along the road to Welton and turn right. Walk through Nether Welton and take the next road on your right to Rose Bridge. The diversion adds only about a mile and a half to your route mileage and could save you a lot of hassle and wet feet.

The official route goes through a narrow gap in the far right hand side bridge wall. It's quite a drop down into the field and, with six narrow steps to negotiate, very awkward when you're carrying a big haversack. Take care.

Follow the river round to a rather overgrown section at the foot of a wooded bank. Here a footbridge crosses a mill race and

Rose Bridge

a stile takes you into an open field. Keep walking along the river bank through a series of fields. One is laid out as an impressive horse jumping course.

Beyond Bog Bridge the path approaches a small wood. You can skirt round the outside if you wish or go through it. The wood can be a pleasant contrast to the open country you have been going through. Your choice may depend on the weather. It might be nice to get out of the sun!

On the other side of the wood, the route crosses a large field, part of the Rose Castle Estate. You can see the Rose Castle buildings to your left. Bishops of Carlisle have lived at Rose Castle since the thirteenth century.

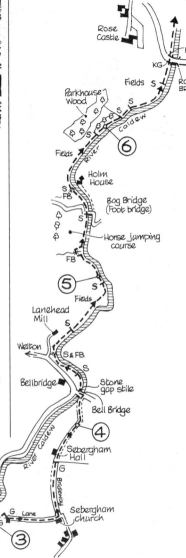

Rose Castle

Cross the road and continue along the river bank, following a sign which says 'Public footpath to Holm Hill'.

The river also floods here at times. If necessary, go up the road to Rose Castle, then take a right turning to Lime House School.

Half a mile downstream of Rose Bridge, the river swings right, but the path continues straight on up a hill. From the top you can take your last lingering look back to the distant Lakeland fells. Misty eyes time.

Continue across the field and skirt the woodland around Lime House School. Cross the end of the school drive and go through a

Lime House School

kissing gate onto a track across a field to Holmhill Farm. Turn right along the narrow road lined with trees and signed 'Bridge End'.

Go past Hawksdale Hall, a fine Georgian house, onto a bridle-way. Keep the wire fences on your left as the bridleway climbs a hill, then turns sharp left into an enclosed lane lined with neat bungalows.

At the end of the lane, turn right and go down the hill on the busy main road into Bridge End. The Fiat filling station sells sweets, drinks and ice cream. The Bridge End Inn sells pub grub and beer.

Cross the bridge opposite the pub on the road signed 'To Dunbar and M6' into the village of Buckabank. Turn right at the first junction you come to and go through a pleasant housing estate.

Turn left at Bishop's Mill, but don't cross the bridge over the mill race in front of you. Instead,

Hawksdale Hall

turn right down a lane alongside
the mill race to Ellers Mill. Pass
the industrial buildings and turn
left at the first junction to White
Bridge.

A choice has to be made here.
Either take the route through
Dalston to Cummersdale on
mostly flat paths with good
surfaces, or follow the southern
river bank through some pleasant
woodland but where the paths are
often very wet and muddy with
some slippery hills to climb. It
depends on your sense of
adventure, I suppose!

Bridge End Inn

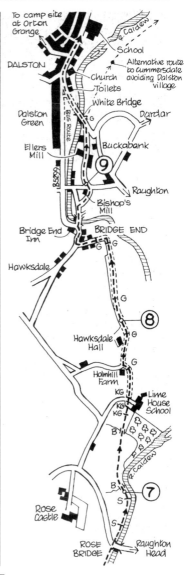

Railway bridge at Cummersdale

Dalston route

Go through Dalston to just beyond the primary school. There turn right down a fenced pathway towards the river. Join a cinder track behind the BLC factory and cross a couple of open fields to a fortified pathway pinched between the river and the railway.

Keep to the fields beside the railway embankment for a straight walk along a remarkably peaceful valley considering how close it is to Carlisle. Over a mill stream, go along a metalled lane and under a railway bridge to the factories at Cummersdale. Cross the footbridge over the river.

Approaching Denton Holme

Southern river bank route

At the end of the lane from Ellers Mill, cross the road and go through a kissing gate signed 'Public footpath to Cummersdale'. Keep to the stream, then bear right along a rough track to a fence. Follow this round to a stile into a small wood. Beyond the wood, cross a footbridge to the river bank. Go through another wood, then cross a stile on your right and follow the fence on your left, avoiding some erosion of the river bank. Head towards the railway line and go through the stone bridge under it. An obvious path joins the Dalston route at the footbridge.

Continue along the river bank until the countryside walk ends at some stone steps into a city suburb street at Denton Holme.

The Caldew, which has grown substantially since first seen close to its source near Skiddaw House, turns away to join the Eden north of the city and eventually flow into the Solway Firth.

For Carlisle city centre, keep on the road you're now on. When it joins a wider one, James Street, turn left up the hill. Pass the public swimming baths, then bear right onto Victoria Viaduct over the railway. Turn left at the traffic lights into Fisher Street, a traffic-free area. At its head stands the pretty pink Old Town Hall and the Market Cross. Congratulations, you've walked The Cumbria Way!

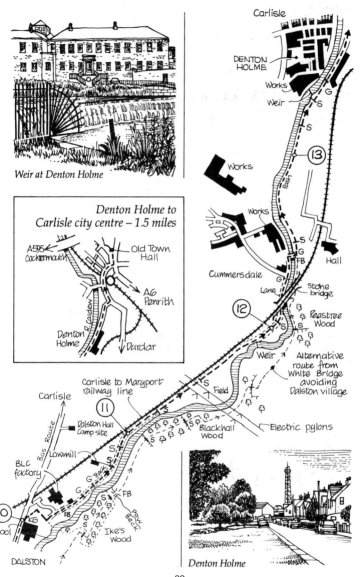

Weir at Denton Holme

Carlisle

DENTON
HOLME

Works

Weir

⑬

Back

Works

Works

Hall

G
S

S

S

S
G
FB

Cummersdale

G

Stone
bridge

Lane

⑫

Peastree
Wood

S

Weir

Alternative
route from
White Bridge
avoiding
Dalston village

Field

S

Electric pylons

Denton Holme to Carlisle city centre – 1.5 miles

A595
Cockermouth

Old Town
Hall

A6
Penrith

Caldew

Denton
Holme

Durdar

Carlisle to Maryport
railway line

Carlisle

⑪

Dalston Hall
Camp site

Bus Route

Lowmill

BLC
factory

G Track

Blackhall
Wood

S

S

G

FB

FB

Pow Beck

⑩

KG

chool

Ike's
Wood

DALSTON

Denton Holme

– 89 –

WALK RECORD

Section 5 - Caldbeck to Carlisle – 15 miles

Date walked

28.02.03

Departure time from Caldbeck	Arrival time at Carlisle
9.15	2.15

Weather conditions   FINE CLEAR DAY.

Notes   OK TO DARSTON THEN
BORING & DULL WALKING TO
FINISH - RUSHED A BIT
TODAY AS BAD WEATHER
COMING IN . MANAGED
5 DAYS OF DRY BRIGHT
WEATHER & DRY
UNDERFOOT
WHO WOULD
THINK IT
WAS FEB.!!

JimWatson

Old Town Hall & Market Cross

arlisle has a long and often violent history. Founded by the Romans to serve the nearby Hadrian's Wall garrison, the city was fought over by England and Scotland for more than three hundred years. The Scots besieged it nine times and Carlisle had four periods of being part of Scotland. Robert the Bruce and Bonnie Prince Charlie both led forces against Carlisle Castle

and Mary Queen of Scots was for a time imprisoned within its massive sandstone walls.

Even today Cumbria's capital city seems closer in character to Scotland than the Lake District. In fact there's little to connect them at all. The Citadel, where the bigamous husband of The Beauty of Buttermere was tried for forgery, forms a gateway to central Carlisle near the railway station, and that's about the only connection there is.

If you want to shop after your long walk, visit The Lanes off Scotch street, though don't expect to be able to replace your worn out walking kit. The shops are very much what you get in any other British city.

Carlisle's rather grand railway station, which once supported seven different railway companies, was built in 1847 by

The Cathedral

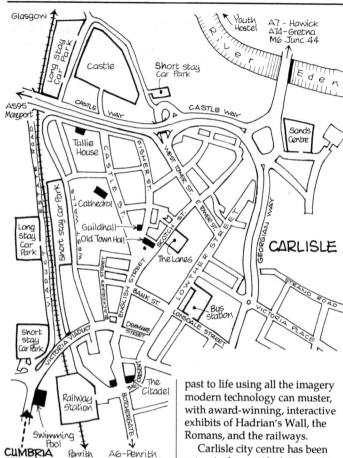

Sir William Tite.

The Cathedral was founded in 1122, with stained glass from the 14th-20th centuries.

Tullie House Museum and Art Gallery brings Carlisle's turbulent past to life using all the imagery modern technology can muster, with award-winning, interactive exhibits of Hadrian's Wall, the Romans, and the railways.

Carlisle city centre has been extensively prettified. Most of it looks very attractive. Other areas, however, look sadly neglected. Venture down Botchergate for example and you may very soon wish yourself back walking the Cumbria Way.

I hope you may quite like that idea anyway.

WHAT TO SEE

Castle Tel: (01228) 591922
Houses Border Regiment Museum.
Open: Apr-Sep, daily 9.30-6.00,
Oct-Mar daily 9.30-4.00.
Tullie House Castle Street.
Tel: (01228) 34781
Open: Mon-Sat 10.00-5.00.
Sun 12.00-5.00.
Cathedral Tel: (01228) 48151/35169
Open: Daily 7.30-6.30.
Guildhall Beside Old Town Hall.
Tel: (01228) 34781
14th Century timber-framed house.
Industrial Carlisle Visitor Centre.
Open: Daily 10.00-5.00.
Old Town Hall Visitor Centre
Tel: (01228) 512444
The *Story of Carlisle*, maps, guide
books, and souvenirs.
Open: Mar-Oct, Mon-Sat 9.30-5.00.
Sun 11.00-4.00.

WHERE TO EAT

Plenty of choice. Shop around.

GETTING THERE

Rail – Good services from
Newcastle, Scotland and the south.
Station enquiries tel: (01228) 44711
Bus – Not so good.
Enquiries tel: (01228) 21038
Air – Carlisle Airport.
Enquiries tel: (01228) 73641
Road – **M6 motorway** junctions 42,
43, & 44. **A596** from West Cumbria.
B5299 from Caldbeck. **A74** from
Glasgow. **A7** from Edinburgh.

TOURIST INFORMATION

Old Town Hall.
Tel: (01228) 512444

WHERE TO STAY

Courtfield House, 169 Warwick Road,
Carlisle. Tel: (01228) 22767

Howard House, 27 Howard Place,
Carlisle. Tel: (01228) 29159

Cournerways, 107 Warwick Road,
Carlisle. Tel: (01228) 29842/21733

Howard Lodge, 90 Warwick Road,
Carlisle. Tel: (01228) 29842

Whitelea, 191 Warwick Road,
Carlisle. Tel: (01228) 33139

Fern Lee, 9 St Aidan's Road, Carlisle.
Tel: (01228) 511930

Kenilworth, 34 Lazonby Terrace,
Carlisle. Tel: (01228) 26179

Tourist Information at Carlisle will find
and book you local accommodation
over the phone for a deposit paid by
cheque or credit card.

Note - This is not a recommended list.
Always phone ahead with your own
requirements.

CAMP SITES

Dalston Hall, A595 near Dalston.
Tel: (01228) 710165

Orton Grange, B5299 near Dalston.
Tel: (01228) 710252

YOUTH HOSTEL

Etterby Road, Etterby, north Carlisle.
Tel: (01228) 23934

THE
ALLERDALE
RAMBLE

FIRST, A WORD ABOUT
LAKE DISTRICT RAIN....

GUIDED
WALK
Meet here

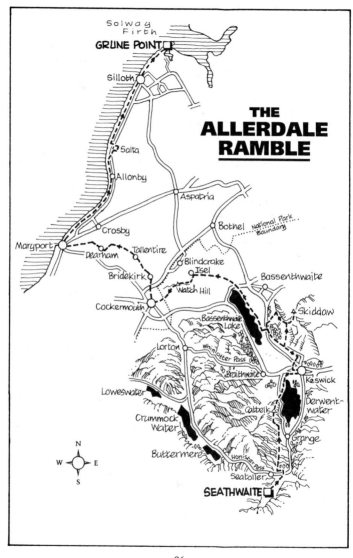

From a quick glance at a map the attractions of the Allerdale Ramble are not obvious. For one thing only half of its 50 miles is in the Lake District. But as with the Cumbria Way, it's not just the scenery that makes a walk interesting. It's the variety and the contrasts.

The Allerdale Ramble has even more contrasts than the Cumbria Way. It starts at Seathwaite, deep in the Lakeland fells, and ends in the flat, wide-open spaces of Grune Point on the Solway Firth. A bigger contrast would be difficult to find.

Along the way you can enjoy one of the most scenic walks in England, from Seathwaite to Keswick; climb Skiddaw, one of only four summits in the Lakes over 3000ft high; visit the stately home of Mirehouse and the tiny, ancient church of St Bega. You can also discover Bassenthwaite Lake and the forgotten countryside to its north; explore the pretty, market town of Cockermouth and valiant Maryport, rising again from industrial decline. Finally, stride along deserted sandy beaches to enjoy the timeless seaside charms of Silloth and the flora and fauna paradise of Grune Point.

Unlike the Cumbria Way, the Allerdale Ramble does not split naturally into equal sections. However, this enables you to make your own programme, taking in the things that interest you most. You can even avoid the towns if you want.

My ideal programme would be:

Day 1: Walk Seathwaite to Keswick (9 miles). Stay overnight at Keswick.

Day 2: Climb Skiddaw (12.75 miles round trip). Stay overnight at Keswick.

Day 3: Walk Keswick to Cockermouth (14.5 miles). Explore Cockermouth. Stay overnight at 'Sundown', just outside the town.

Day 4: Walk Cockermouth to Crosscanonby (10.5 miles), exploring Maryport on the way. Stay overnight at East Farm, Crosscanonby.

Day 5: Walk Crosscanonby to Grune Point (14 miles). Stay overnight at Silloth.

The Allerdale Ramble has much to enjoy. There's a lot more to Cumbria than just the Lake District National Park.

Maps required:
OS Landranger 1:50 000 Sheet 85 – Carlisle and the Solway Firth.
Sheet 89 – West Cumbria.
Sheet 90 – Penrith, Keswick and Ambleside.
These cover all the route.

The English Lakes, 1:25 000 Outdoor Leisure, North West sheet covers the National Park section in greater detail.

Seathwaite

With 130 inches of rain a year, the hamlet of Seathwaite is famously the wettest inhabited place in England. It also offers food, accommodation, camping and grass-verge car parking. A track goes south from Seathwaite up to Styhead Pass and Big Fell country.

The Allerdale Ramble starts at the north east corner of the farm-yard. A sign indicates 'Path to Borrowdale via Thorneythwaite'.

Follow the obvious route along the fell bottom. As you approach Thorneythwaite Farm (B&B), swing right onto a metalled track which leads to the main road.

Cross the road to a path signed 'To Longthwaite' and cross Folly Bridge into the wood. Turn left to follow the river upstream. Behind the holiday centre building, turn right up the clear fellside to join a track coming from the car park at Seatoller.

Climb for a short stretch until the track swings left, then turn off right through a gate onto a steep, eroded fell path. The path soon levels out to give a wonderful view of the route ahead, rolling across the bracken-clad hills above Borrowdale to the tooth-like stump of Castle Crag.

Borrowdale

– 98 –

Suggested day's walk

Borrowdale bus from Keswick to Seatoller. Walk up road to Seathwaite. Walk Allerdale Ramble back to Keswick – **11 miles**

Accommodation in Borrowdale

Seatoller Farm, Seatoller.
Tel: (017687) 77294.
Gillercombe Guest House.
Tel: (017687) 77602.
Seathwaite Farm, Seathwaite.
Tel: (017687) 77394/77284.
Thorneythwaite Farm, Seatoller.
Tel: (017687) 77237.
Peat Howe, Longthwaite.
Tel: (017687) 77346.

Camp sites

Chapel House Farm.
Tel: (017687) 77602.
Stonethwaite Farm.
Tel: (017687) 77234.

Youth Hostel

Longthwaite.
Tel: (017687) 77257.

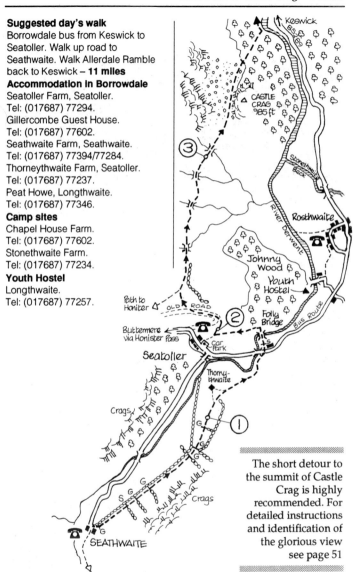

The short detour to the summit of Castle Crag is highly recommended. For detailed instructions and identification of the glorious view see page 51

Go down the rough track between the spectacular Low Scawdel scree slope and Castle Crag into the wood. Keep to the beckside path through the wood to Gowder Dub, a lovely place to rest, on the River Derwent. Turn left along the river bank onto a track which joins the metalled lane to Hollows Farm. This part of the route is also part of the Cumbria Way.

Turn right to go to Grange-in-Borrowdale for accommodation, cafes, a gift shop, bus stop, telephone and public toilets; all in a beautiful alpine setting.

If for some explicable reason you want to avoid Grange, turn left up the lane to Hollows Farm and walk along the fell bottom. If you then want to take the level lake shore route to Keswick, join the road out of Grange and follow the Cumbria Way description beginning on page 53.

For the more adventurous Catbells routes, turn left up the lane to Hollows Farm and go through a gate behind the farmhouse onto a track. Over a footbridge, swing left away from Grange to wind uphill past Highclose Woods on your right to a gate onto open moorland.

Turn right, keeping left of the wall behind Ellers and avoiding some possible muddy places, to a sign which indicates 'Permissive path to Catbells and the road'. Beyond the wall, follow set posts behind the small wood above Manesty, then go along a fence to a stile.

Turn sharp left here and climb to the end of the wall where a

Geological change from craggy volcanic to smooth slate above Hollows Farm

sign indicates 'Catbells High Path'.

The path soon divides. For Catbells summit, fork left and climb up the steep fell path - aided in places by a handrail - to the cross-roads of paths on the plateau of Hause Gate. Turn right up the heather-covered slope to the little rocky summit and exquisite views of Derwentwater and Newlands.

For a more gentle route without much climbing, take the right fork behind a plantation wall to a stone seat, a memorial to the writer, Sir Hugh Walpole, who lived at Brackenburn, the house in the trees. The path descends to the road at an old quarry, then climbs again to a part path, part slate track with splendid lake views, eventually joining the motor road at the end of the Catbells ridge.

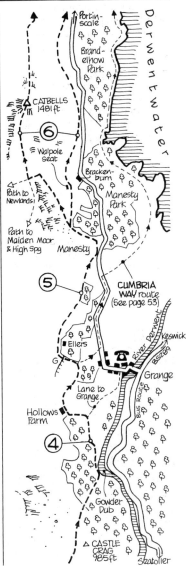

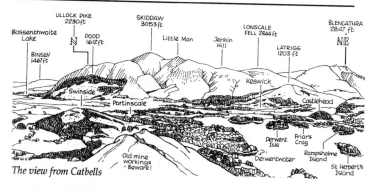

The view from Catbells

The descent from Catbells summit and the traverse of the broad, grassy ridge to Hawes End is delightful but needs care in the steeper sections. The final stretch zig-zags steeply down to the road and may require subtle use of hands and backside to bolster your sense of security.

Keep to the path and avoid walking on the slippery grass slopes.

Walk down the road, cross a cattle grid to the tight Z-bend in the road and bear right through a gate past a sign pointing back to 'Catbells, Brandelhow and Tewthwaite'. Go through another gate onto a short, rough path signed 'To the Launch Pier'. At the junction with a track follow the sign 'Public footpath to Portinscale'.

The partly-surfaced footpath goes through a wood and over footbridges to a forestry road.

Portinscale

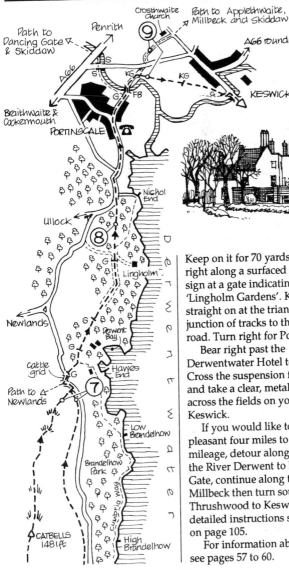

Lingholm

Keep on it for 70 yards, then fork right along a surfaced path to a sign at a gate indicating 'Lingholm Gardens'. Keep straight on at the triangular junction of tracks to the motor road. Turn right for Portinscale.

Bear right past the Derwentwater Hotel to the river. Cross the suspension footbridge and take a clear, metalled path across the fields on your right into Keswick.

If you would like to add a pleasant four miles to your day's mileage, detour along the bank of the River Derwent to Dancing Gate, continue along the road to Millbeck then turn south through Thrushwood to Keswick. For detailed instructions see the map on page 105.

For information about Keswick see pages 57 to 60.

From Crosthwaite Church on the outskirts of Keswick take the path up the hill by a row of oak trees to the left of the school. Continue between large houses and down a hill to the bridge under the old railway. Cross the busy A66 (carefully!) and two fields to Thrushwood.

Go over the Keswick to Carlisle road and through a small wood onto a track up an open field. Skiddaw looms straight ahead. At the end of the wire fence, bear left into an enclosed (often muddy) pathway which opens out onto the rising road through Applethwaite. Great views back to Derwentwater.

Turn left at the telephone box and left on a signed footpath into a small yard. Go over a stile into an open field. Keep walking across the slope, follow the signs around the farm and turn right into the hamlet of Millbeck. Carry on to the road junction, turn left and then right to a sign saying 'Public footpath to Skiddaw'.

If you decide not to climb Skiddaw, carry on along the road from Millbeck to the path into Dodd Wood at Dancing Gate.

The route from Portinscale follows the bank of the River Derwent. Cross the river at some farm buildings and go up the lane towards Dodd Wood. Go over the Keswick to Carlisle road, turn left and walk along the roadside for a short distance to where a sign indicates the narrow road right to Millbeck. Just into this road a lane goes off left into Dodd Wood.

Applethwaite

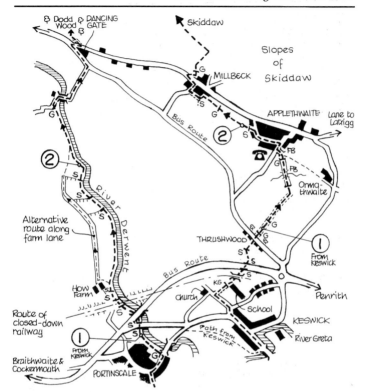

Suggested day's walk

A) Keswick, Millbeck, Skiddaw, Bassenthwaite Lake, Castle Inn, bus back to Keswick – **13 miles**

B) Keswick, Dancing Gate, Dodd Wood, Mirehouse, Bass Lake, Castle Inn, bus back to Keswick or stay at Bassenthwaite – **9 miles**

C) Route B to Bass Lake plus Watch Hill, stay at Cockermouth – **14 miles**

Accommodation

Bassenthwaite Hall Farm.
Tel: (017687) 76279.
Green Farm, Bassenthwaite.
Tel: (017687) 76361

Parkergate, Bassenthwaite.
Tel: (017687) 76376.
Low Grove Farm, Millbeck.
Tel: (017687) 75763.
Lonnin Garth, Portinscale.
Tel: (017687) 74095.
Lake View, Portinscale.
Tel: (017687) 73249

Camp sites

Robin Hood House, Bassenthwaite.
Tel: (017687) 76334.
Lake Dist. Caravans, Bassenthwaite.
Tel: (017687) 76298/76068.
Scotgate Park, Braithwaite.
Tel: (017687) 78343.

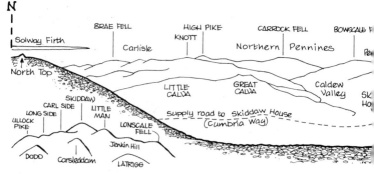

The Skiddaw massif

This route is in my opinion the finest way to climb Skiddaw. At first the path through stony bracken is unclear but you can't go wrong, just head straight up the fellside. It is unremittingly steep but well compensated for by the glorious view south.

At the 1500 feet level you reach the sparkling quartz crags of White Stones. Then a remarkably straight path rises easily through the heather to the grassy plateau summit of Carl Side. Swing right for the well-worn path across the scree slope to Skiddaw summit.

Descend by reversing your steps to Carl Side, then simply walk along the edge soaring right to Ullock Pike. A wonderful walk, safe, but take care near the start where the path has fallen away. The views, especially to Bassenthwaite, are tremendous.

As the Edge begins to level out, watch for a path going off left down to a fir plantation. Follow the fence back towards Keswick and finally bear right into the wood to emerge on the road near Ravenstone Hotel.

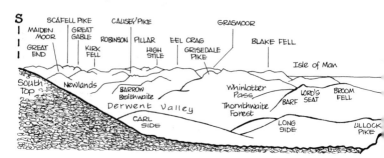

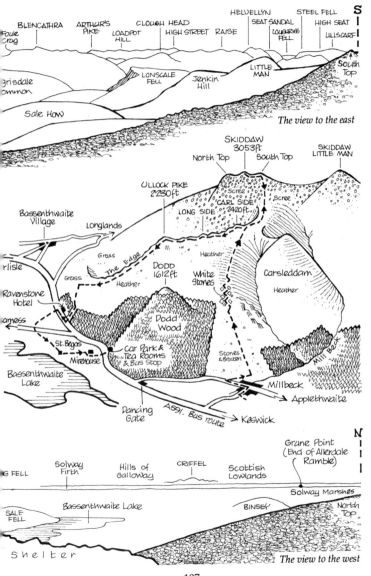

The view to the east

SKIDDAW 3053ft
North Top — South Top
SKIDDAW LITTLE MAN

ULLOCK PIKE 2230ft
CARL SIDE 2420ft
LONG SIDE
Scree
Scree

Bassenthwaite Village
Longlands
Grass
The Edge
Grass
Heather
Heather
White Stones
Carsleddam
Heather

Carlisle
DODD 1612ft

Ravenstone Hotel
Dodd Wood
Stones & Bracken

amess
St. Begas
Mirehouse
Car Park & Tea Rooms & Bus Stop
Mill Beck
Stones & Bracken

Bassenthwaite Lake
Dancing Gate
A591. Bus route → Keswick
Millbeck
Applethwaite

The view to the west

G FELL
Solway Firth
Hills of Galloway
CRIFFEL
Scottish Lowlands
Grane Point (End of Allerdale Ramble)
Solway Marshes

N

SALE FELL
Bassenthwaite Lake
BINSEY
North Top

Shelter

The view to the west

From the lane, climb through the wood to a clearing from where a well-defined path zig-zags to a wide forestry track. Follow this northwards to a path which descends steeply to Dodd Wood tea room and car park.

Cross the road and go down the lane on the south side of Wood Cottage. This takes you past Mirehouse and through fields to St Bega's church.

Mirehouse is the epitome of the English country manor house, once the home of noted nineteenth-century literary figure James Spedding. Tennyson was a visitor and used Bassenthwaite as a setting for his *Morte d'Arthur*.

The elegant house is open to the public with members of the Spedding family often on hand to show you round. Clean your boots first!

St Bega's church stands in

Wood Cottage

glorious isolation beside the lake, possibly the most romantic spot in all Lakeland.

From St Bega's, swing right around Highfield Wood into another small wood. For the next half mile of small woods, pasture and a farm track the straight path utilises two plank footbridges, four stiles and three gates before joining the minor road to Scarness at the corner of a copse.

If you're coming from Skiddaw, turn right for 200 yards

Mirehouse

past the Ravenstone Hotel, then turn left through a signed gate opposite the hotel name board. Descend past some very tall Scots Pine trees and cross a pasture into a small wood. Continue through a series of four gates to an electricity sub-station beside the Scarness road. Turn right along the road to

join the route from Dodd Wood.

If at this point you want to return to Keswick rather than carry on to Castle Inn, cross the road to a track which takes you to St. Bega's church. Continue up the lane past Mirehouse to the Dodd Wood car park and the bus stop for Keswick.

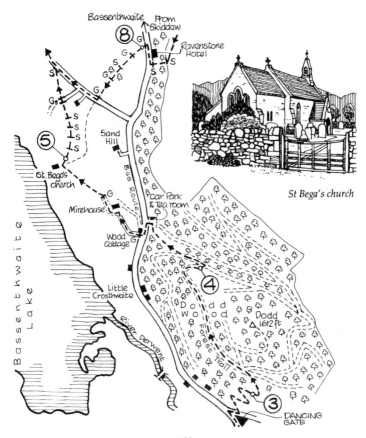

St Bega's church

Bassenthwaite Lake and Ullock Pike

Walk 250 yards along the Scarness road and go over a stile on your left just before a bridge. Cross a tiny field to another stile onto rough ground by a ditch. Cross a footbridge and continue beside a fence to a stile, south of Broadness Farm, onto the lake shore at Bowness Bay.

The next mile is a wonderful walk, on soft turf mainly, with superb views of Skiddaw, Ullock Pike and the Thornthwaite Fells across the lake.

Bassenthwaite Lake is almost four miles long and three quarters of a mile wide. One of the largest lakes, but with a depth of 70 feet it is also one of the shallowest.

Apart from the A66 road rumbling along its west side, the shores are relatively unspoilt. Power craft are banned and most of the southern end is given over exclusively to wildlife.

With many fences and becks running down to the lake, you will have to negotiate at least ten stiles and two footbridges before arriving at Scarness Bay.

Go past the landing stages and take a path past a caravan site in the wood on your right to the hamlet of Scarness.

Turn left along the minor road and bear right along the drive past two houses on your right.

Scarness Bay

Go through the gate next to Scarness Farm and down the hill on a track to a bridge and a gate.

Continue through more gates and cross a bridge over a walled beck. Follow the raised north bank for a short distance, then cut across a reed-covered open field to a wood on your right.

Go through the wood using single plank bridges over a couple of ditches. Emerge onto a clear path through pastures, but with woods hiding the lake to your left.

A variety of stiles and footbridges brings you to the B5291. Armathwaite Hall gates are 200 yards up the road to your right.

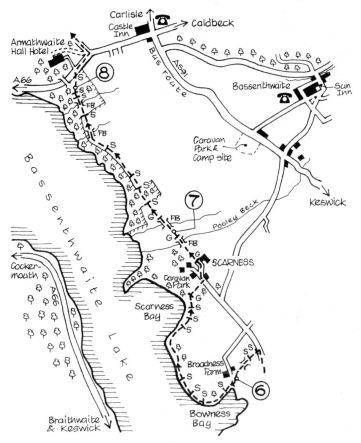

The lane behind Armathwaite Hall

For Castle Inn and the Keswick to Carlisle bus stop, keep walking on the B5291 road .

For Bassenthwaite village, turn right at Castle Inn for a short distance, then take the first road turning on your left.

To continue on the Allerdale Ramble, turn left down the lane next to Armathwaite Hall entrance, where a sign indicates

The lane from Long Close Farm

'Trotters and Friends Animal Farm'.

At the end of the tarmac road follow the sign indicating 'Public footpath to Isel'.

The next two miles along Buckholme Lonning to Long Close Farm are packed with delights, though the going under foot can be very muddy. As ever, the high quality scenery makes up for any inconvenience down at feet level.

The River Derwent, meandering through the woodland and pastures, makes an interesting companion. Broad and powerful after rain, the river rests during drought, displaying great banks of smooth, delicately-coloured pebbles washedup amongst cool, deep pools of sparkling, clear water. The Skiddaw massif still lords it in the south, but in the few miles from Bassenthwaite Lake the landscape has softened and become more rural.

This almost forgotten area of Cumbria, away from the tourist hot-spots and noisy roads, has about it a most attractive, timeless quality, where time seems not to have just slowed down but to have never existed at all. If you think that the attractions of Cumbria begin and end with the Lake District, prepare to be surprised from now on!

Go through a gate at Long Close Farm onto a tarmac lane andkeep straight on at the T-junction along a country road to Isel Bridge.

Isel Bridge

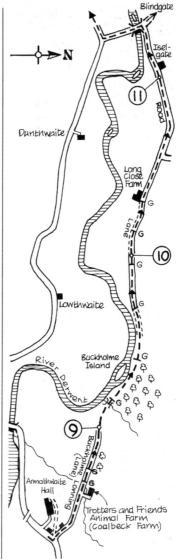

The alternative route avoiding Cockermouth starts here. For details see page 116.

Even if you intend to cross the bridge to Watch Hill, the next big viewpoint on the route rising tree-covered across the river to your right, it is worth first making the short detour right to have a look at Isel.

There's no village or even a huddle of buildings that could be called a hamlet, just a mill and a couple of cottages next to Isel Hall, a large, mainly sixteeth-century mansion built onto an even older pele tower overlooking the river.

Attractive enough, but it's St. Michael's Church, beautifully set at an ancient crossing place on the river, which draws the crowds. Most of the present building is Norman with a chancel arch and roofing timbers little changed since construction in 1130.

The track to Watch Hill

Cross Isel Bridge and pass a small layby and a gate giving access to the riverside and a Countryside Commission footpath around the perimeter of the Dunthwaite Estate. Continue up the hill on the road and turn right at the T-junction.

After about 250 yards on the gently-rising road, turn off left through a gate onto a forestry track sign-posted 'Public Bridleway'.

Straight and well surfaced, the track climbs gradually through bracken and gorse bushes. Half a mile into the wood, the main track swings left through a steel barrier. You should bear right here onto a higher track climbing more steeply into the wood.

There's now a good view north across Isel to the limestone outcrops around Blindcrake. The wood itself is very pleasant too, not the usual dense conifers, but mixed varieties of trees with some substantial beeches.

Leave the wood over a stile onto a grassy hillside. Turn left and climb to the hilltop. Walk along the crown of the hill to bring Skiddaw into view.

No cairn marks the summit of Watch Hill. At only 770 feet it is low in elevation but high in view assimilation. This extends without interruption from Skiddaw in the east, across the lonely Lorton

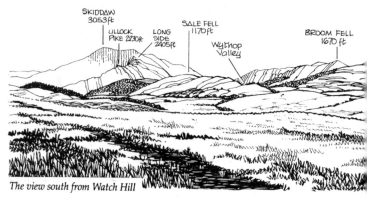

The view south from Watch Hill

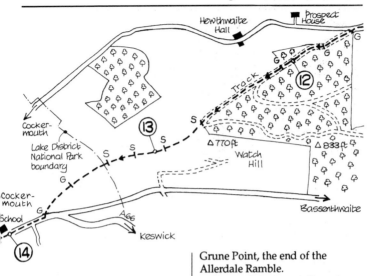

Fells, bulky Grasmoor and the Buttermere Biggies to the south, the gleaming Solway Firth in the west and further north, just visible against the four white towers of Annan power station,

Grune Point, the end of the Allerdale Ramble.

Descend down a well-used path to Cockermouth, initially keeping close to a solid, stone wall, then across an open field and through wide farm gates to the old main road. Turn right into Cockermouth.

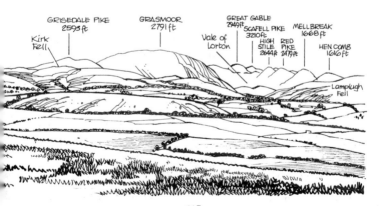

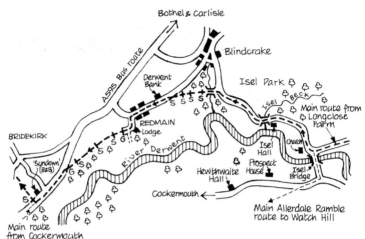

to a stile with a signpost pointing back to 'Public footpath Blindcrake – Isel road'.

Go over the stile into a country road and turn left along the road into the hamlet of Redmain.

Turn left at a sign indicating Redmain Lodge, then swing right through a gate onto a farm track. When the track turns left, keep straight on up a terraced path, and left of a rocky knoll.

With woods on your right, cross two stiles and go across a pasture with rocky outcrops but no visible path. A stile and a gate gives access to a lay-by on the A595 Cockermouth to Carlisle road and a great view across Cockermouth to Buttermere.

Turn left along the broad grass verge for about 600 yards, then cross the road to a stile in a stone wall signed 'Public footpath to Bridekirk'.

I f for some unexplicable reason you want to avoid Watch Hill and the attractive market town of Cockermouth, there is an alternative route. This can also be utilised to complete a circular walk beginning and ending at Cockermouth.

Begin the detour at Isel Bridge. Turn right along the road and bear left at the Y-junction past Isel Hall and the Almshouses. Cross the bridge over Isel Beck and climb uphill on a delightful, wooded country road.

Follow the signpost 'Public Footpath Redmain' left into Gill Wood onto a narrow path crossing a pretty footbridge over a rushing stream, then a stile into a field with many tree stumps. Keep climbing across the hillside, going over two stiles and past a spring

WALK RECORD

Seathwaite to Cockermouth			

Route Seathwaite – Keswick

Miles 9	**Total mileage** 9	**Start time**	**Finish time**

Weather

Notes

Route Keswick – Dodd Wood – Armathwaite Hall – Cockermouth

Miles 14	**Total mileage** 23	**Start time**	**Finish time**

Weather

Notes

Route Keswick – Skiddaw – Armathwaite Hall

Miles 11.75	**Total mileage** 20.75	**Start time**	**Finish time**

Weather

Notes

Route Armathwaite Hall – Cockermouth

Miles 6	**Total mileage** 26.75	**Start time**	**Finish time**

Weather

Notes

Route

Miles	**Total mileage**	**Start time**	**Finish time**

Weather

Notes

Market Place

A vicious loop in the National Park boundary excludes Cockermouth from the Lake District. Sensibly then, the town largely ignores the tourist jamboree and looks westward to the industrial plants along the coast for its prosperity.

Cockermouth was founded in the twelfth century when a castle was built at the junction of the River Derwent and River Cocker. Robert the Bruce destroyed part of it, but it survived a famous siege during the Civil War. The castle is now mainly a ruin, only rarely open to the public. One wing is a private residence.

Ever since the castle was built a brewery has snuggled up to its massive west wall. Though high-tech, Jennings modern brewery still follows traditional methods. Visitors are welcome. No, you can't test the product.

Cockermouth once had over 40 industrial sites, many of them water-powered along the Cocker and Derwent. Corn, wood and cotton were the mainstays with tanning and hat-making also significant trades. Later came shoes, silks and threads.

Sadly, all of it has gone. Many of the old buildings remain, altered for other uses, but still well worth seeking out.

The town's broad main street, where Hiring Fairs were once held, is now lined by trees and comfy old-fashioned shops. Kirkgate and Market Place are very attractive with some handsome Georgian houses giving the town an air of gentility.

The oldest part, pre-1600, is at the bottom of Castlegate, where an alleyway leads to the Toy and Model Museum. All the big names are on show – Hornby,

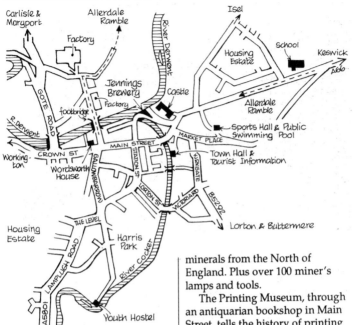

Meccano, Triang, Scalextric.

Castlegate House Gallery at the top of Castlegate shows paintings by living local artists.

The Mining Museum, part of a gift shop, displays over 200 minerals from the North of England. Plus over 100 miner's lamps and tools.

The Printing Museum, through an antiquarian bookshop in Main Street, tells the history of printing from 1800.

Cockermouth has many surprises. Look out for the United Reform Church in Main Street and the Grecian Villa built in 1847 by hat manufacturer Thomas Wilson.

Main Street

Remember Fletcher Christian, the *Bounty* mutineer? He was born near Cockermouth, at Eaglesfield, in 1764. Incredibly, John Dalton, who developed the atomic theory, was born in the same village two years later. It must be something in the water. Four years after that, in 1770, William Wordsworth, England's greatest poet since Shakespeare, was born in the finest house in Cockermouth.

It was built in 1745 by Joshua Lucock, High Sheriff of Cumberland. John Wordsworth, a solicitor, worked as land agent for James Lowther, one of the richest landowners in the north. The house went with the job. All five Wordsworth children were born here. When their mother died, eight year old William moved to Penrith with his sister Dorothy. Both of them later wrote affectionately about their childhood in Cockermouth.

John Wordsworth died five

Town Hall

years after his wife. He is buried in All Saints churchyard.

The sandstone church, which replaced a 1711 building burnt down in 1850, has an impressive 180ft-high spire. An east window commemorates Wordsworth.

Kirkgate is good for an evening stroll with some good views across the town from Mackreth Row. Also try Hope Park for pleasant walks along the riverside.

Wordsworth House

WHAT TO SEE

Wordsworth House Main Street.
Tel: (01900) 824805
Open: April to October,
Mon-Sat, 11.00-5.00.
Jennings Brewery Brewery Lane.
Tel: (01900) 823214
Phone for tour times.
The Printing House Main Street.
Tel: (01900) 824984
Open: February to November,
Mon-Sat, 10.00-4.00.
The Toy Museum Market Place.
Tel: (01900) 827606
Open: Every day, 10.00-5.00.
Mining Museum Main Street.
Tel: (01900) 828301
Open: Mon-Sat, 10.00-5.00.
Castlegate House Castlegate.
(Opposite entrance to the Castle)
Tel: (01900) 822149
Open: March to December, daily
except Sun & Thu, 10.30-5.00.

GETTING THERE

Bus – Good services from Keswick
and Workington. Less good from
Carlisle.
Enquiries tel: (01946) 63222
Road – **A66** west from Keswick and
north from Workington. **A595** from
Carlisle. **A5086** from Egremont.

WHERE TO EAT

Over The Top, Kirkgate.
Tel: (01900) 827016

Norham Restaurant, Main Street.
Tel: (01900) 824330

Cheers, Main Street.
Tel: (01900) 822109

WHERE TO STAY

Wordsworth Hotel, Main Street,
Cockermouth. Tel: (01900) 823591

Albany House, Windmill Lane,
Cockermouth. Tel: (01900) 825630

Castlegate Guest House, Castlegate,
Cockermouth. Tel: (01900) 826749

Rose Cottage, Lorton Road,
Cockermouth. Tel: (01900) 822189

The Old Vicarage, Lorton Road,
Cockermouth. Tel: (01900) 828505

Evening Hill House, Brigham Road,
Cockermouth. Tel: (01900) 827980

Note - This is not a recommended list.
Always phone ahead with your own
requirements.

CAMP SITES

Violet Bank, Simonscales Lane,
Cockermouth. Tel: (01900) 822169

Wyndham Holiday Park, Old Keswick
Rd, Cockermouth. Tel: (01900) 822571

Graysonside Farm, Lorton Road,
Cockermouth. Tel: (01900) 826972

YOUTH HOSTEL

Double Mills, Cockermouth.
Tel: (01900) 822561

TOURIST INFORMATION

Town Hall, off Market Place.
Tel: (01900) 822634

Bridekirk

Go down a narrow road midway along Cockermouth main street and cross the metal footbridge over the River Derwent to a grass recreation area and car park. Continue along the side of the old factory building and turn sharp right at the end through a gate with a footpath sign onto a dirt lonning.

Follow the path uphill over a series of stiles. Go over the brow of the hill, then downhill with a fence on your right. Cross a field to a stile with a footpath sign giving access to the A595 Cockermouth to Carlisle road.

Turn right for 200 yards along the broad grass verge, then cross the road to a stile in a wall signed 'Public footpath to Bridekirk.' Go up the field and over the brow of the hill to another stile. Keep right of a wall to a third stile then turn right to a sign pointing back 'Public footpath to Carlisle road'.

Go through a gate and turn right along a narrow road. Turn left at the junction into Bridekirk, a peaceful place with no public amenities. Continue through the village. At the bottom of the hill, 500 yards beyond the church, turn off the road through a gate into a field on your right.

Climb diagonally across the rocky bank to your left. Go over a stile at the top and pass a copse of trees. Use two stiles to cut across the next field then swing left to follow a wall down to a farm track into Tallentire.

The compact village has excellent B&B accommodation and a homely pub, the Bush Inn. If you stay overnight take a stroll out of the village to Tallentire Hill for some fabulous views and if you're really lucky a spectacular sunset over the Solway Firth.

Gate into field near Bridekirk

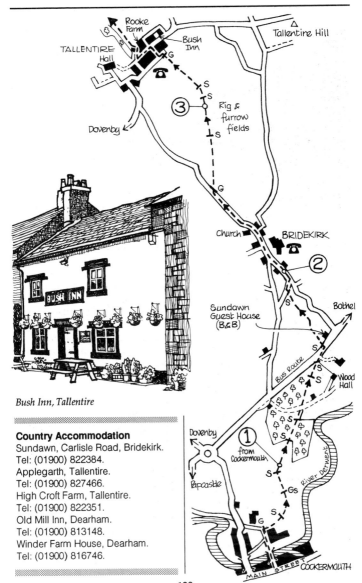

Bush Inn, Tallentire

Country Accommodation
Sundawn, Carlisle Road, Bridekirk.
Tel: (01900) 822384.
Applegarth, Tallentire.
Tel: (01900) 827466.
High Croft Farm, Tallentire.
Tel: (01900) 822351.
Old Mill Inn, Dearham.
Tel: (01900) 813148.
Winder Farm House, Dearham.
Tel: (01900) 816746.

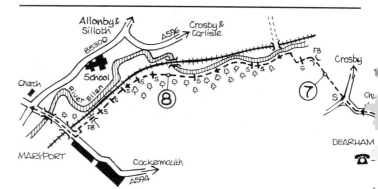

Follow the signpost on Tallentire main street indicating 'Public footpath to Row Brow' along the short lane into Rooke Farm. Go between the farm buildings onto a farm road.

If you are going to Dearham and Maryport, swing left after about 200 yards across a narrow field to walk around the boundary of a wood.

If you want to avoid Dearham and Maryport, keep straight on along the farm track and follow the alternative route as detailed on page 126.

For Dearham, turn left around the end of the wood to a gate by Park Lodge. Turn right onto the farm road and keep on it over cattle grids to Low House. Go past the farmhouse onto a tarmac road. At the junction with the main road, turn left into Row Brow on the outskirts of Dearham.

Old Mill Inn, Dearham

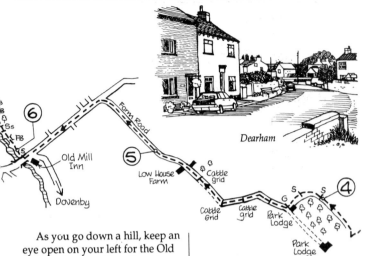

Dearham

As you go down a hill, keep an eye open on your left for the Old Mill Inn by a road junction. Go over a stile across the road from the inn, signed 'Public footpath to Parish Church'.

Follow the path beside Row Beck into a wood. Look out for a bridge over the beck which goes through garden allotments and up a steep lane to emerge near the church in Dearham, a sprawling, coal-mining village.

Go up the village street to the Globe Inn. Turn right at the road junction along a narrow, country road out of the village. At the next junction go over a stile signed 'Public footpath to Maryport'.

Follow the track for about 500 yards across the open elevated field with a view before you of Maryport and the Solway Firth. The next downhill stretch is narrow and will probably be muddy, but things will improve

when you get to the River Ellen.

The next mile or so into Maryport is a very pleasant walk. Some of it runs alongside the broad Ellen, some on a wooded terraced path, high above the river. A series of stiles, steps, stepping stones and small bridges keeps the going interesting.

At the corner of the last of a number of narrow fields, cross a footbridge onto a well-trod path which passes between the back gardens of a modern housing estate and the railway line.

After about 250 yards the path emerges beside the main road near a sign that says you have just walked 'Public footpath No. 104044' from Dearham.

Turn right along the main road into Maryport.

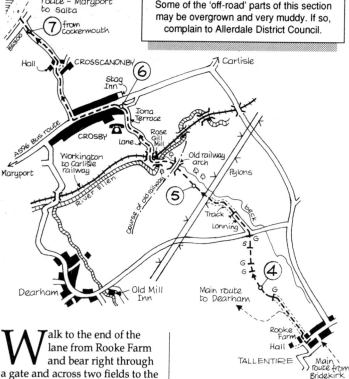

Note!
Some of the 'off-road' parts of this section may be overgrown and very muddy. If so, complain to Allerdale District Council.

Main Allerdale Ramble route – Maryport to Salta

⑦ from Cockermouth

Hall CROSSCANONBY

Stag Inn ⑥ Carlisle

Iona Terrace

CROSBY Rose Gill Mill Lane

Workington to Carlisle railway Old railway arch

Maryport Pylons

A596 Bus route

River Ellen Course of old railway ⑤ beck

Track Lonning

⑤ S G
G G ④ G

Dearham Old Mill Inn Main route to Dearham

Rooke Farm Hall

TALLENTIRE Main route from Bridekirk

Walk to the end of the lane from Rooke Farm and bear right through a gate and across two fields to the top of a low hill. Go over a fence and down the hill to the left edge of a fir copse.

Cross the Dearham road into a lonning. Go through a gate at the end onto a cattle track. Keep parallel to the beck across a scrubby area, then descend to go under a disused railway arch. Swing left round a hillock and cross the River Ellen by a footbridge to Rose Gill Mill.

Go over the railway and climb the steep lane to Iona Terrace.

Swing left into Crosby main street opposite the Stag Inn. Take the next road on your right through Crosscanonby to join the main route from Maryport.

Accommodation
East Farm, Crosscanonby.
Tel: (01900) 812153.

WALK RECORD

Cockermouth to Maryport

Route	Cockermouth – Maryport		
Miles 8.5	**Total mileage**	**Start time**	**Finish time**
Weather			
Notes			
Route			
Miles	**Total mileage**	**Start time**	**Finish time**
Weather			
Notes			
Route			
Miles	**Total mileage**	**Start time**	**Finish time**
Weather			
Notes			

GOING FAR ?

The Romans were first to develop this part of Cumbria. They built the fort of Alarna on the cliff top, part of the coastal defence system of Hadrian's Wall. The Battery, an old Royal Naval Reserve station beside the fort remains, now houses the Senhouse Roman Museum, one of the country's oldest and most important private collections of Roman relics, altars and sculptures. Humphrey Senhouse developed the harbour and town from the village of Ellenfoot and in 1838 renamed it Maryport after his wife.

By 1857, 3000 ships were using the harbour and the annual coal exports from local mines reached half a million tons. The railway came in 1845 generating even more trade. Senhouse dock opened in 1884 to ship locally-made railway lines worldwide.

Unfortunately, the dock was too small to take the large new steamships and the west coast trade moved to Liverpool and Bristol. Maryport's long and painful decline had begun.

The deep mines were soon worked out and the iron works closed in 1927. Unemployment reached 80% in 1931. The final blow fell during 1961 when the docks were closed.

But by then workers had turned to the modern industrial plants springing up along the Cumbria coast and Maryport became largely a dormitory town.

Now with inspired planning and heavy financial investment the sunshine of tourism begins to brighten the shabby Maryport streets. Fleming Square, still cobbled with what Charles Dickens called 'fossilised kidneys' and lined by picturesque Georgian and Victorian houses, has been restored to its former

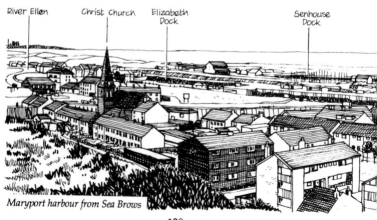

River Ellen   Christ Church   Elizabeth Dock   Senhouse Dock

Maryport harbour from Sea Brows

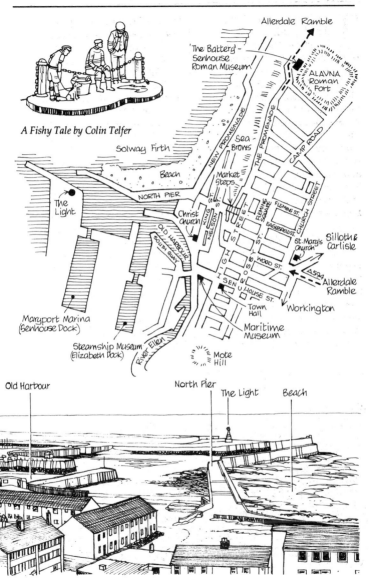

A Fishy Tale by Colin Telfer

Allerdale Ramble

'The Battery' - Senhouse Roman Museum

ALAVNA Roman Fort

Solway Firth

Beach

Sea Brows

THE PROMENADE

CAMP ROAD

NEW PROMENADE

NORTH PIER

Market Steps

The Light

OLD HARBOUR

Christ Church

NELSON ST.

KING ST.

HIGH STREET

FLEMING SQUARE

FLEMING ST.

EAGLESFIELD ST.

CHURCH STREET

St. Mary's Church

Silloth & Carlisle

SOUTH QUAY

WOOD ST.

SENHOUSE ST.

A594

Allerdale Ramble

Town Hall

Workington

Maryport Marina (Senhouse Dock)

Steamship Museum (Elizabeth Dock)

River Ellen

Maritime Museum

Mote Hill

Old Harbour

North Pier

The Light

Beach

glory as the old town market place and goose fair site.

L.S. Lowry enjoyed sketching the harbour area and it is here that £25 million is to be spent. Derelict land has been cleared, silted-up docks dredged, a marina opened and housing built. An hotel, restaurants, shops, a sports hall and a heritage park are to come.

Elizabeth Dock now harbours what's left of the Maryport fishing fleet, and the Maryport Steamship Museum. This 'museum' has only two exhibits: *The Flying Buzzard*, a restored Clyde tug built in 1951, and *Vic 96*, a naval supply ship. Both vessels are worth a tour.

A Lowry-like sculpture at the harbour entrance is the work of local ex-miner Colin Telfer who records the fast disappearing quarrying and mining traditions. He uses local hematite ore as a medium, the only person in the world to do so.

Maryport Maritime Museum stands on the first plot of land that Humphrey Senhouse developed

Maritime Museum

in 1749. Old photographs tell the history of the port and there are items relating to *Bounty* mutineer Fletcher Christian and Thomas Henry Ismay, the founder of the White Star Line, builders of the ill-fated *Titanic*. Ismay was born at Maryport in 1837. The building also houses the Tourist Information Centre.

George Stephenson, who planned the Maryport to Carlisle railway, and the novelists Charles Dickens and Wilkie Collins stayed nearby at the Golden Lion in Senhouse Street.

Maryport has a good promenade and a decent sandy beach. Despite an often foul-looking sea it's a good place to wander and perhaps to wonder if the old town will ever recover its old vitality.

Take a walk along the south pier to The Light, erected in 1846 and now one of the oldest iron-built lighthouses in the world. Carry on to the end of the stone pier, but take care – the sea can be very, very angry here.

Fleming Square

WHAT TO SEE

Maritime Museum Senhouse Street, Maryport. Tel: (01900) 813738
Open: Easter to October,
Mon-Sat 10.00-5.00, Sun 2.00-5.00.
Senhouse Roman Museum
The Battery, Maryport.
Tel: (01900) 816168
Open: July to September,
every day, 10.00-5.00.
Steamship Museum Elizabeth Dock, Maryport Harbour.
Tel: (01900) 815954
Open: Easter to October,
10.30-4.30, except Thursday.
Town and Harbour Walks Excellent leaflet from Tourist Information Centre will lead you to all the best bits.

GETTING THERE

Rail – Infrequent service from Carlisle and Workington on the scenic Cumbria Coastal Line.
Enquiries tel: (01539) 720397
Bus – Reasonable services from Cockermouth, Workington, and Carlisle. Sparse service from Silloth.
Enquiries tel: (01946) 63222
Road – A596 from Carlisle and Workington. **A594** from Cockermouth. **B5300** from Silloth.

TOURIST INFORMATION

Maritime Museum, Senhouse Street.
Tel: (01900) 813738

NOTE

Maryport has no Camp Site and no Youth Hostel.

WHERE TO STAY

Ellenbank Hotel, Birkby.
Tel: (01900) 815233

The Retreat Hotel, Birkby.
Tel: (01900) 814056

Waverley Hotel, Curzon Street.
Tel: (01900) 812115

Golden Lion Hotel, Senhouse Street.
Tel: (01900) 812663

Ellenside Guest House, 17 Station St.
Tel: (01900) 815440

10 Selby Terrace.
Tel: (01900) 813595

11 Selby Terrace.
Tel: (01900) 817150

2 Borriskill, Ellenborough.
Tel: (01900) 813527

Note - This is not a recommended list. Always phone ahead with your own requirements.

WHERE TO EAT

The Retreat, Birkby.
Tel: (01900) 814056

Waverley Hotel, Curzon Street.
Tel: (01900) 812115

Barney's, 64/66 Curzon Street.
Tel: (01900) 812532

Harbour View, 2 South Quay.
Tel: (01900) 817573

The Battery – Senhouse Roman Museum

Leave Maryport along the elevated promenade overlooking the harbour at Sea Brows.

Go past the distinctive Victorian building which houses the Senhouse Roman Museum and take the surfaced path undulating across old mine workings to join the Old Promenade at almost sea-level, 100 yards before Bank End Farm.

The wide, open aspect across the Solway, a complete contrast to the sometimes claustrophobic skyline of the Lake District, some good, bracing walking.

Beyond the Golf Course you can walk along the beach – hard going on the legs after a while – or crack on along the rough grass strip between beach and road.

The Saltpans at the foot of Swarthy Hill date back to medieval times and were used to extract salt from the sea by evaporation. Salt used to be a valuable commodity and was taxed until 1824. There are picnic tables at the excavation and you can climb steps up the 100 foot high hill to admire the view.

Village shop, Allonby

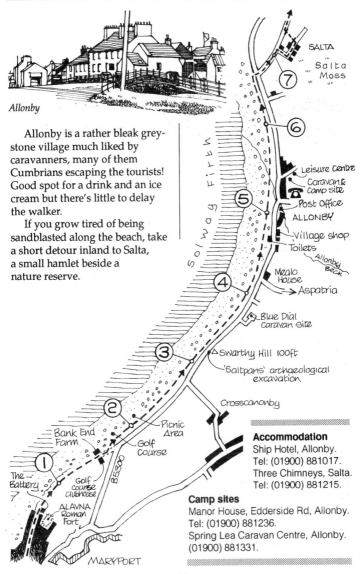

Allonby

Allonby is a rather bleak grey-stone village much liked by caravanners, many of them Cumbrians escaping the tourists! Good spot for a drink and an ice cream but there's little to delay the walker.

If you grow tired of being sandblasted along the beach, take a short detour inland to Salta, a small hamlet beside a nature reserve.

Accommodation
Ship Hotel, Allonby.
Tel: (01900) 881017.
Three Chimneys, Salta.
Tel: (01900) 881215.

Camp sites
Manor House, Edderside Rd, Allonby.
Tel: (01900) 881236.
Spring Lea Caravan Centre, Allonby.
(01900) 881331.

Mowbray

At the end of the tarmac road at Salta go through a gate onto a track. Continue across fields through two more gates and turn right along the minor road to the Lowther Arms at Mawbray. Turn left at the triangular green and walk through the village back to the beach.

Resume walking north along Mowbray Bank, a 300 yard wide strip of undulating grassy sand dunes with car parks, litter bins and numerous sandy footpaths.

BENGAIM 1250 ft

The Scottish hills across the Solway Firth

Lane into Silloth

Keep walking north along dunes, pebble shore or sands. The sand between Beckfoot and Blitterlees goes out for almost a mile at low tide.

Camp site

Rowanbank Caravan Park, Beckfoot. Tel: (016973) 31653.

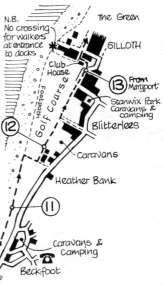

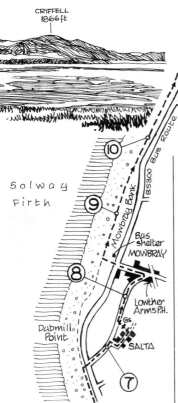

When you come to the southern boundary of Silloth Golf Course, you can **either** carry on walking along the beach to the pier at the other side of the course and turn right up a narrow path to join a tarmac road. Go past the docks to the club house and central Silloth.

Or you can turn inland here along a fenced-in path. This takes you round the edge of the golf course past a number of caravan sites to the B5300 road. For Stanwix Park camp site, turn right for 500 yards along the road.

For central Silloth walk straight along the main road at the end of the lane, then cut through by the Club House and turn right into Criffel Street.

WALK RECORD

Maryport to Silloth

Route   Maryport – Silloth

Miles 12	**Total mileage**	**Start time**	**Finish time**
Weather			
Notes			

Route

Miles	**Total mileage**	**Start time**	**Finish time**
Weather			
Notes			

Route

Miles	**Total mileage**	**Start time**	**Finish time**
Weather			
Notes			

THESE NEW BOOTS ARE SO
LIGHT I HARDLY KNOW
I'M WEARING THEM

JimWatson

Criffel Street

Silloth was originally part of the grange farm of Holme Cultram Abbey. When the abbey was dissolved in 1538 land sold off as farming packages grew into a sizeable settlement.

The biggest growth came after the railway line linking the manufacturing centre of Carlisle with the sea arrived in 1856. Silloth Dock, opened in 1858, is still used, mainly to ship cattle and grain. A flour mill still flourishes by the Green.

Streets were laid in a grid-iron pattern similar to those at Maryport and Whitehaven and Silloth began to develop as a holiday centre as well as a port. The old cobbled streets remain and much of the Victorian elegance, albeit slightly faded and weather beaten. Silloth is still a

considerable holiday resort. Caravans and holiday centres abound and the town has become a favourite get-away-from-it-all place for hardy Cumbrians whose country idylls have become over-run by tourists.

Grune Point is the get-away-from-it-all place for people who want to escape Silloth. On the east side of the mile-long headland the vast mudflats of Skinburness Marsh stretch away across Moricambe Bay to the estuaries of the Waver and Wampool. Hedges and trees only survive in sheltered spots around the bay.

The upper Solway is one of the largest inter-tidal habitats in Britain, a vital link in the chain of west coast estuaries for wintering wildfowl and waders. The Grune was made a SSSI in 1988 to

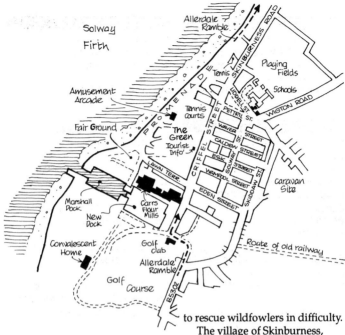

protect the Natterjack toads, invertebrates and rare plants, including the bloody cranesbill and the Isle of Man cabbage.

The wartime lookout shelter marking the end of the Allerdale Ramble was rebuilt in Buddist style as a memorial to four local people who drowned while trying to rescue wildfowlers in difficulty.

The village of Skinburness, once a port owned by the monks of Holme Cultram Abbey, is now almost a suburb of Silloth. Edward the First gathered a fleet of 50 ships here for the invasion of Scotland in 1300. The port was destroyed by a storm in 1301.

The Promenade

WHAT TO SEE

Apart from the Holiday Centres, the attractions of Silloth are mainly outdoor and natural. The sunsets across the Solway can be very spectacular. And they don't cost you a penny.

GETTING THERE

Bus – Service from Carlisle via Wigton. Sparse service from Maryport.
Enquiries tel: (01946) 63222
Road – **A595, A596** & **B5302** from Carlisle.
B5300 from Maryport.
A595 & **B5301** from Cockermouth.

WHERE TO EAT

Rose Barn Restaurant, Green Row, Silloth. Tel: (016973) 32707

Sunset Inn, Stanwix Park Leisure Centre, Silloth. Tel: (016973) 31671

Solway Holiday Centre, Skinburness Road, Silloth. Tel: (016973) 31236

Susanna's Pantry, Eden Street, Silloth. Tel: (016973) 42541

Friendly's Cafe, Station Road, Silloth. Tel: (016973) 31319

All the hotels have public restaurants.

YOUTH HOSTEL

Silloth has no Youth Hostel.

TOURIST INFORMATION

The Green. (Limited winter opening)
Tel: (016973) 31944

WHERE TO STAY

Nith View Guest House,
1 Pine Terrace, Silloth.
Tel: (016973) 31542

4 Pine Terrace, Silloth.
Tel: (016973) 31794

57 Wampool Street, Silloth.
Tel: (016973) 32026

Golf Hotel, Criffel Street, Silloth.
Tel: (016973) 31438

Queen's Hotel, Criffel Street, Silloth.
Tel: (016973) 31373

Skinburness Hotel, Skinburness.
Tel: (016973) 32332

Nook Farm, Beckfoot. (Between Silloth and Allonby on the Allerdale Ramble) Tel: (016973) 881279

Note - This is not a recommended list. Always phone ahead with your own requirements.

CAMP SITES

Moordale Caravan Park, Blitterlees.
Tel: (016973) 31375

Seacote Caravan Park, Skinburness Road. Tel: (016973) 31121

Stanwix Park Leisure Centre, Green Row. Tel: (016973) 31671

Tanglewood Caravan Park, Causewayhead. (Wigton Road) Tel: (016973) 31253

Cote Lighthouse

This final stretch begins at Silloth docks. Walk north along the promenade, passing the lifeboat station, the Cote Lighthouse and the Longhouse where Sir Walter Scott once stayed. At the road turning right to Skinburness, keep straight on on through a gate onto the Grune.

You can now walk on the soft shingle beach or take the inshore grass path which meanders through rough pasture and dense gorse bushes. Four white cooling towers at Annan power station in Scotland are prominent across the Solway. The maze of pylons and wires seen across Moricambe mud and sand flats are at Anthorn in England.

A World War Two observation post marks the end of the Allerdale Ramble.

Return to Skinburness first along the stony beach beside the extensive mudflats, then on a track, and finally a road, which turns sharp right to the hotel.

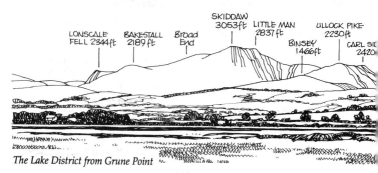

The Lake District from Grune Point

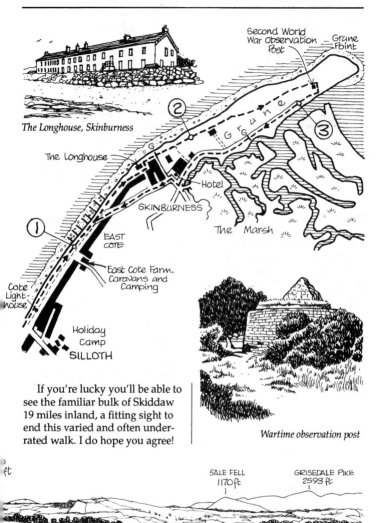

The Longhouse, Skinburness

Second World War Observation Post

Grune Point

The Longhouse

Hotel

SKINBURNESS

The Marsh

EAST COTE

East Cote Farm. Caravans and Camping

Cote Lighthouse

Holiday Camp
SILLOTH

Wartime observation post

If you're lucky you'll be able to see the familiar bulk of Skiddaw 19 miles inland, a fitting sight to end this varied and often under-rated walk. I do hope you agree!

ft

SALE FELL
1170 ft

GRISEDALE PIKE
2593 ft

WALK RECORD

Grune Point circuit

Route   Silloth – Skinburness – Grune Point – Skinburness

Miles	4	**Total mileage**	**Start time**	**Finish time**

Weather

Notes

DID YOU **HAVE** TO BRING **EVERY** GUIDE BOOK THERE IS ?

Allerdale District Council,
(Planning Dept. and Tourism Section)
Allerdale House, Workington
CA14 3YJ. Tel: (01900) 604351

South Lakeland District Council,
Stricklandgate, Kendal.
Tel: (01539) 733333

Carlisle City Council,
(Countryside Officer), Civic Hall,
Rickergate, Carlisle CA3 8QG
Tel: (01228) 23411

Lake District Special Planning Board
(Park Management Service)
Murley Moss, Oxenholme Road,
Kendal LA9 7RL
Tel: (01539) 724555

Cumbria Wildlife Trust,
The Badger's Paw, Church Street,
Ambleside LA22 0BU
Tel: (015395) 32476

English Nature, Blackwell,
Bowness-on-Windermere LA23 3JR
Tel: (015394) 45286

Friends of the Lake District, No. 3,
Yard 77, Highgate, Kendal LA9 4ED
Tel: (01539) 720788

Youth Hostels Association,
PO Box 11, Matlock,
Derbyshire DE4 2XA
Tel: (01629) 825850

BBC Local Radio:
North 95.6 FM. 756 AM.
West 95.6FM. 1458 AM.
South 96.1 FM. 837 AM.

Travel Link – Information on all bus
and rail services throughout Cumbria.
Tel: (01228) 812812

Stagecoach Cumberland – Bus
services in the National Park.
Tel: (01946) 63222
or write to:
Stagecoach Cumberland, PO Box 17,
Tangier St, Whitehaven CA28 7XF

Rail Enquiries: (01539) 720397
or write to: Travel Link, Cumbria
Cumbria Council, Citadel Chambers,
Carlisle CA3 8SG

Train, Bus & Coach hotline
Tel: (01891) 910910

Lake District Weather –
Fell conditions and general forecast.
Tel: (017687) 75757

Publications:
*Western Lakes & Coast
Accommodation Guide* – Available
from Tourist Information Centres at
Cockermouth Tel: (01900) 822634
Keswick Tel: (017687) 72645
Maryport Tel: (01900) 813738
Silloth Tel: (016973) 31944

*Keswick and N. Lakes – where to stay
and what to do* – From Keswick TIC.

Caravan & Tent Guide – From any
Lake District TIC.

Cumbria Way accommodation –
Leaflet from Ulverston TIC.
Tel: (01229) 587120